Teacher-Poets Writing to Bridge the Distance:

An Oral History of COVID-19 in Poems

Edited by Dr. Sarah J. Donovan and Carolina Lopez

This 2021 publication is made possible, in part, by the Oklahoma Oral History Research Program and Oklahoma State University Library.

ISBN 978-0-9998768-1-7

TABLE of CONTENTS

TABLE of CONTENTS

TABLE of CONTENTS

TABLE of CONTENTS

INTRODUCTION

The idea of preserving the voices and experiences of teachers who navigated a new reality due to the COVID-19 global pandemic was the starting point of the project Teacher-Poets Writing to Bridge the Distance: An Oral History of COVID-19 in Poems. This oral history project emerged from a celebration of National Poetry Month in 2020 on Ethical ELA, a public website for teachers to read and write poetry and share and discover poetry lessons for their classrooms. Over the thirty days of April 2020, 50 teachers from 22 states wrote nearly 1500 poems.

After writing poetry online for thirty days together, several teachers noticed that this body of poetry held experiences and perspectives necessary to the historical record of the COVID-19 pandemic. Teachers' voices needed to be heard and documented. And so we proposed an oral history project to document the shared and diverse experiences that emerged through and around the intersection of writing poetry and teaching during this unprecedented pandemic. To offer agency and reciprocity to the process, we knew it would be important for the teacher-poets to interview each other for this project, so fourteen of the teacher-poets became teacher-researchers, facilitating the oral history interviews through the poems the teachers chose to share, poems that they thought best represented their experiences living and teaching during the early days of the pandemic.

This anthology offers readers the poems shared across the 39 collected oral histories: 166 poems. We extracted the poems from the transcripts to show the line breaks and stanzas intended by the teacher-poets. In the margins of the pages, the white spaces, this anthology also holds the meaningful connections and the sense of community that developed during the interviews where teacher-poets witnessed one another's lives.

The oral history interviews are available for public access at Oklahoma Oral History Research Program where you can listen to the teacher-poets' emotions, reactions, and insights elicited by reading their poetry. By doing this, revisiting poems written a year prior, teachers re-witness, with perspective offered only by time, the impact of COVID-19 on them as teachers and on education more broadly.

Feelings of uncertainty and anxiety were two of the most common reactions to the sudden closings of schools. Some felt the need to show their best face and attitude towards the chaos. While feeling uncertain of the future, teachers had to give their best for their students. Every school district had its own set of guidelines and procedures to follow during the pandemic. While some teachers were fully grateful and agreed with their state's rules, other teachers had to struggle with the decision-making that was taken in their designated schools. Inequity was a theme throughout the interview process, too. Teachers shared how many of their students were not given adequate technology and materials for the transition to online learning. Therefore, teachers had to figure out how to fulfill their students' and own at-home learning needs based on what was available. Some teachers shared how teacher-parent relationships developed through increased communication and support given during this transition while others lost touch with families and even students altogether.

In several oral histories and poems, there is an increase in self-care. Teachers shared how the pandemic helped them slow down their daily routines and focus on their mental and physical health. Writing poetry was therapeutic -- the routine, the audience, the creativity. Many of the poems here are not about teaching at all. They are about being.

The poems in this anthology are arranged chronologically by the date they were archived. You can learn more about the teacher-poets in the section called "Teacher-Poets." We hope you will bear witness to their lives through these printed words and then again through their voices and silences recorded in the video oral history interviews online at the Oklahoma Oral History Research Program.

The Process ~
Shaun Ingalls

First one up, always.
Find a pair of clean shorts and a t-shirt –
nobody to impress during quarantine.
Start the pot of Folgers – gotta prime the pump.
It's an eight-cup day.
Delete emails while the coffee brews.
How much of one's life is spent pressing miniature trash cans?
Okay, okay, okay, just a minute!
Fill a travel cup and take the dog on walk #1 –
lots of dog-walking during quarantine.
Toast a bagel. Not really hungry, but I do it anyway –
lots of unnecessary eating during quarantine.
Sit down, alone, at the dining room table slash home office slash second
grade classroom –
no large groups dining during quarantine.

Moving Day ~
Shaun Ingalls

Today I have to put the contents of 2019-2020
into dozens of cardboard boxes,
number them, put my name on them,
and hope they find me again.
This double-wide box has seen things:
puppet shows, musicals, lip syncs, poetry orations,
standardized testing, open houses, prom night invites,
observations, staff meetings, staff development,
tears of joy, tears of frustration.
This year didn't end as planned.
The seniors didn't get to finish together.
The juniors didn't get to AP stress together.
We didn't get to sign our yearbooks together.
So, stop by next year and visit me.
Take in a big whiff of that new-classroom-smell,
and we'll try to make up for lost time.

Incorporating *Mooses* by Ted Hughes ~ Shaun Ingalls

The beast's temperament is an enigma,
goofy howling while driving home on the first day.
Moose sound the same, only a few octaves lower.
The jig was up when he screamed and hollered for a couch rescue.
Walking down the hallway, I raced to see what's the matter.
House alive with worry and concern. Then his limber
frame leaped into the air and onto the floor like an Olympic gymnast,
manipulative monster.
Is this how it's going to be?
Lost forever in those mud-brown eyes,
In the bushy white eyebrows that furrow and judge,
the tilt of the head and slight flick of a too small pink tongue,
forest of cotton snout tangles comically horizontal after a nap?

Gathering Worms ~
Shaun Ingalls

Grandpa held the red plastic flashlight
with his left hand
and shined it over the black earth,
his little worm box in his right hand
the green metal edges
barely visible in the dark.
Kneeling down I could see
slimy brown bodies sticking out an inch or two.
Quickly I snatched the slimy beast
and felt the muscle pull back into the black loam.
With the silver trowel,
I scooped a column of earth
under the worm
to prevent its escape.
The writhing and wrenching
never stops
until it burrows into the bottom
of the worm box
only to be seen again
when pulled out
to conceal a silver hook
at the end of my line.

Come Worship With Us ~
Abigail M. Woods

Do you ever wonder why congregations sing?
Why even the most devout have a moment
Of self-infatuation – an existential crisis
– In the pit of a Sunday sermon?

My god, I am certain that even the most
Ardent skeptic could be convinced of the almighty
In the shoulder-to-shoulder GA parish,
In the audience to a midnight worship.

When was the last time you felt God's presence?
Stood face-to-face with the king-of-kings
Competing with the holy vibrations of industrial
Subwoofers and amps – a steeple for all and one

I am convinced that God is a bass drop.
The first wave of a monumental night
Baptizing the flock of sinners before it,
Washing away the grime of a religious experience.

On Alice Paul at the Seaward-Belmont House ~ Abigail M. Woods

"There will never be a new world order
Until women are a part of it."

Alice Paul looks like my great-grandmother –
Or more accurately, Mamaw looked like her.
The white home-perm curls and flared nostrils
Lips always pursed, ready to comment on
Your posture or how one of the boys better
Take her fishing or she was going to switch
Their asses like when they were children.
Eyes that dealt discipline on a silent platter,
Alice probably avoided photographs if she could.
She probably laughed with a wide-open mouth,
Her head tossed backwards. She never missed the
Chance to tell you her opinion. Mamaw, though,
Was a different kind of feminist. The kind that
Leaves her husband when he hit her, pregnant and
Full of a life. I imagine her sailor mouth chattering
Under her breath as she walked, belly and all, to
The doorstep of her mother's home. She would
Drink her red beer, and cut her friends hair until
She had a beauty-parlor to call home – and there,
She'd drink water. She raised four boys that weren't
Hers – and it should have been five – because it was
The right thing to do. She always made sure everyone
Was fed and had a place to sleep. She slept in a bed
On her own and married a man because he took pictures
Of her instead of the mountains cascading around her.
Alice Paul looks like my great-grandmother –
Or more accurately, Mamaw looked like her.

Walmart ~
Abigail M. Woods

"You
will have
to enter
on the other
side." Pointing to the
right. The man explodes.
"Screw you" he spits at me. "It
is city-mandated" *I am not
your door-mat,* I mean to say, *I am
essential, critical, at-risk worker.*

For Unelavnhi, the Great Spirit ~
Abigail M. Woods

Before god moved into the Americas
Built his white brick house and burned crosses
In our neighbors yards, the Cherokee's worshipped
Here. The rise and fall of the Appalachians,
The colossal peaks of the Great Smokies,
The plentiful and green gullies and valleys.
There are still bones were my ancestors lay,
Under your plantations and your highways,
Under your malls and your domesticated feet,
Are the flattened mounds of unrestful souls.
In the spring, I imagine you can still hear
Their stomps, their prayers, their turtle shells shaking
From their feet with the beat. The Cherokee's were
Not meant to be sedentary. I think that's why
I long for exploration. They had the earth to worship,
To wander, to love. I imagine if I laid down on this
Grassy slope, the trees would stretch their
Roots to my arms, hold my hands as they
Washed me in the thick dirt of the Mother.
This is where I belong – in the light of the day,
Under the same skies my people once followed,
But I will not stay.

From the massive oak trees who's century old
Roots dig into the ground deeper than the
Stakes of my tent could ever fathom, from
The silver and turquoise fingers that plant
My gardens and beg for them to yield their
Peppers, from the crackle and pop of my kitchen
When there are ten people between me and the
Door. I can hear them
Iyuno unelavnhi wadiyi nasgi nanahwunvgi,
nasgi hawinaditly duyugodv nahnai.

Translation:
If the creator put it there,
It is in the right place.

Three-For-One ~
Abigail M. Woods

A laundry mat on wheels
One side clean, the other side dirty
An hour to school and an hour
Back to mom's. Forty-five minutes
To my bed and fifteen to dad's.
I no longer live my life this way.
The learning curve has taken awhile,
But I do not need to hoard sweatshirts
In my floorboard. I take my wallet in
When I get home. I don't leave
My life in the car.
I no longer live that way.

I called it home for most of my life.
A white brick building turned cream
From years of red-dirt dust. Velvety
Red carpets, a nursery, a hallway with
A kitchen, three rooms for study, and
A children's place at the back.
I had, at one point, begged for
My own, but when I finally moved
Out, I left it there, in the bedroom
Of a girl that once spent her Sunday's
At service and her Wednesday's at group.
I don't want my bible anymore.

I was always a water baby. Maddie
Tells me this is because I am a
Gemini but let's be honest, I just love
The feeling of the creek rushing over
Me. I love the campgrounds, the
Fire roasted jalapeno hot dogs, and
The overwhelming smell of sunscreen.

We went on our own trip a few years
Back. I realized it wasn't the
Place that I loved so much,
But the people. And the people
Aren't the same anymore. Some got
Divorces, and some got sober, some
Had some kids and others left because
They didn't. I was too young to
Realize then that the creek was more
Than a creek.

Egyptian Rat Screw (Or, ERS) ~
Abigail M. Woods

Samuel slams his palm on the table,
Roaring with his victory like a lion over his prey.
Zach's body shakes with laughter, aggressively
Rattling the table. This game, not life or death,
Yet still so crucial to the livelihood of this moment.
Richard is pouting, half-asleep on the couch.
Logan is swirling the green apple wine in her glass
As if there is a cheese that could pair with a jolly-rancher.
She's watching the escalation unfold. Sammy, gloating, pulls
His stack from the tabletop and into his deck, shuffling
To get them all straight, and each of us lean back down
Into position. Sam flips his card and the chaos ensued, again.
Seven of clubs,
Two of diamonds,
King of hearts,
Two of diamonds.
My hand sends ripples through the table as it lands on its target –
Unobstructed. I grab my stack and laugh, staring Sam down.
As previously discussed, this is my game. Zachary cackled, "watch it,
Samuel, you'll summon the beast." He reached over to pat my head.
I start to defend myself from the accusations but the
Red head in the kitchen is having none of it, screeching
"You have a scar from it on your hand, Abigail!"
She whips her body around the corner to stare me down
As if to say, "Abigail, be real here, you're the most competitive person
I've ever met." Flashing before my eyes, I realize that I am happier
In this moment than I have noticed in a while. Sam's still throwing
Taunts onto the wobbly coffee table, and the coffee table is
Questioning whether it will make it through another round of this
Ridiculous game.
These are the people I live for

Where I'm From ~
Abigail M. Woods

I am from dogwoods,
From tree swings and haybales.
I am from crisp green rolling hills
(Overgrown, full of life
It smelled like fresh morning dew.)
I am from the creek-side lawn chair,
The rushing waters
Whose rippling waves haunt my body
Deep in my dreams.
I am from four-wheeler tracks and route-66,
From massive oak trees and blackberry bushes.
I am from the take-it-or-leave-it's
And the five-days-a-week's,
From sun-up to sun-down.
I'm from a red-dirt diamond
With stark-white chalk
And three chances to make it mine.
I'm from Sonic Drive-In's and Spook Light Road,
Sunday service and catfish dinners.
From the bed of a white F-150, filthy and smiling
Snow-cone victories
The bat my father kept from childhood.
In the catalogs under mom's bed
Three 3 weatherproof containers
Each labeled with
A child's name.
I'm from the homerun balls –
Indoctrinated in a younger generation –
Skills of a family tradition.

Almost Asleep ~
Kimberly Johnson

pitch black dungeon dark except for
his screen beam of scrolling
against the haint-proof-blue headboard
eyelids fluttering lazily to the sounds
of drift-on-a-dinghy verge of the
edge of a deep sleep forest
where the gnashing of the
terrible teeth of the wild things
on the fringes of the wild rumpus begins
with the whirring blur of a white noise fan
feverish scritch-scritch circling of Schnauzer Fitz,
feet-sheet-scratching to Shanghai
rumble of thunder as we slumber under the
refrain of pelting rain
grumbling growl of Schnoodle Boo
the king of all wild things
who's snoozing too

Detail of Sapelo River ~
Kimberly Johnson

your marsh and river at dawn and dusk
ever-changing palette of brilliant hues,

a back I scratched on novice skis,
arm I tickled casting lines, nets, shells;

you picked up the dinner check:
deviled crab, steamed shrimp, fried fish,

and lulled me in a dock hammock as I listened
for playful dinnertime dolphins,

an empty mollusk shell now –
priced far less than all you've given.

Paint Chips ~
Kimberly Johnson

smooth sailing days of spring
walking the blank canvas of
the dirt road less traveled
smelling summer squash seedlings
and fresh-squeezed tulips
ambling home for a front porch swing
cup of chamomile tea
steeped in fireflies
and waterfalls

Barnyard Concert at Dusk ~
Kimberly Johnson

stadium of tiered strains
crickets getting on key
off-key bleating goats
sound-boosting rooster straining in
heckling-cackles from the hens
melodic symphony of songbirds
grunty strumming backbeat pig
headbang-drumming woodpecker
string-section grasshoppers' lilting cadence
high-trilling tree frogs
windchimes ring
porch swing chain keeping tempo
as we sway
to this cacophonous
harmonious
sunset serenade

Six Feet Away ~
Andy Shoenborn

There you are,
posing in the tall grass,
wearing a purple shirt made of silk,
and looking, without knowing,
at a version of your future self.

In the present,
I look into the hazel eyes
of my eighteenth year.

I was so sure.
I was all-knowing.
I couldn't wait to escape into
the promise of
adulthood.

I took it all for granted.

We all do, I suppose,
when we have nothing but
time and dreams.

Now, at forty-four,
in a time of quarantine,
I see myself posing
for a senior picture
I never wanted and
wonder aloud for my students.

What of their senior photos?
Some wanted.
Some not.

What of their prom?
Graduation?
Concerts?
First kiss?
Last dance?

Last
chance?

What will they remember
in the COVID-stolen remnants of
a finish line called
Senior Year?

I hope they find time
to pose in the long grasses
near where they live and
capture memories like
fireflies in a glass jar.

I hope they don't
take this time
for granted.

Just because the world
is on pause doesn't mean
they won't look back
on this time for the
rest of their lives.

They will.

I hope, when they do,
they are able to
smile and laugh
in the face of the thief
that stole their inheritance,
and do it, of course,
from a safe distance —
six feet away.

Photo Credit: Susan Jane & Donald P. Goostrey of RBG INC.

Earth Day Presence ~
Andy Shoenborn

Shhh! Breathe. Be still. Enjoy. Silence.
Seek benevolence.
Chirping birds share songs and poems.
Safe at home.
Croaking frogs calling out their love.
Voices rise above.
A cacophony: Earth Day love.
Stop and listen for sounds of Earth.
Pause for a day – your right of birth.
Seek benevolence. Safe at home. Voices rise above.

I See You ~
Andy Shoenborn

I see you, writers,
bringing yourself to the page.

I see you, poets,
unshielded,
taking down walls,
breaking barriers,
and sharing pieces of yourself.

I see you, Glenda,
in your words,
your wisdom, and
your wit. You amaze.
You inspire. Thank you.

I see you, Anna,
celebrating brothers,
celebrating verse, and
celebrating others. You embolden.
You spark. Thank you.

I see you, Michelle,
taking in NYC,
through a window, and
writing beautiful words. You shine.
You impress. Thank you.

I see you, Jennifer,
sharing your words,
in verse and prose,
in nurturing comments. You hearten.
You motivate. Thank you.

I see you, Donnetta,
writing in Texas and
lending your gift
to the page, for us. You influence.
You shine. Thank you.

I see you all,
Stacey and

Mo and
Susie and
Shaun and
Allison and
Alexa and
Malachi and
Paige and
Robin and
Denise and
Gayle and
Kim and
Margaret and
Padma and
Jennifer.

For all those named
and those I missed,
I see you all.

Unshielded,
taking down walls,
breaking barriers,
and sharing pieces of yourself.
I see you, poets.

Bringing yourself to the page –
I see you, writers.

And, I see you, Sarah,
creating spaces for words,
inviting others to be brave,
speaking to the writer
in each of us, leading the way,
encouraging us to embrace our
own sense of #verselove.

Thank you,
thank you,
thank you,
a million times,
thank you for showing
us how to stretch our wings,
so we too might believe
we can fly.

The Other Side of Now ~
Susan Ahlbrand

The slowdown that came with COVID 19
Was a much-needed respite if you know what I mean.
The cause and the reason--to avoid death and avoid the spike--
were not positive but the outcomes are things that I like.

At home with my family, hanging out and having fun
Instead of in the car and constantly on the run
We play games and play cards and cook meals together
We all go outside to simply enjoy the nice weather.

I'm a teacher so I'm still working and making some money
For those who are not this work stoppage is not funny.
All day, I sit at the table staring hard at a screen
Hoping to still reach each student, each confused, antsy teen.

All around our house are others tapping into to Wifi
Two college students, one high school sophomore and two more teachers do try.
We're all trying to grab normal, to move forward in school
While trying out every kind of new technological tool.

My husband is the designated shopper because he hates to stay down
Each day he finds a reason to journey out into the town.
We've cooked more at home this month than all the previous years
ANd those of us over 21 have tried all sorts of new beers.

Daily schedules are wonky, interaction is low
We try to wear face masks wherever we go.
Sweatpants and no make-up have become quite the norm.
Closer bonds with our families we've tried hard to form.

Jigsaw puzzles we've worked and games of euchre we've played
I know we will look back on the memories we've made.
These times have been scary, the sacrifices have been great.
But it will all be worth it, of that one can't debate.

We'll flatten the curve, we'll keep a number from dying
All the while trying to figure out when the politicians are lying.
On the other side, when we're back to "normal" we'll see.
We were given the chance to become new you's and new me's.

What really matters is certain to shift
Back into the chaos, I'm sure many will drift.
But this is our chance after we had no chance but to stop.
To reclaim a life that leaves us feeling on top.

Should we keep going, going and going some more?
Should we keep competing with others, trying to keep score?
Should we sit on the bleachers at ballparks on Sunday?
Should we walk right on by neighbors with nothing to say?

No, we should slow down and live life at our own pace.
We should worry about us and not others to race
We should keep the Sabbath holy and spend time with our clan
We should visit with others, make that our main plan.

Corona forced a slowdown, billions of dollars have been lost
But we can use this as a time to find things that don't cost.
Find things that do matter, make us smile and feel loved.
To help those around us and praise God up above.

On the other side of this thing, whenever that comes
Don't go back to normal, don't return to being bums.
Hold on to the good from this time we've lived through
And come out as a much better version of you.

Stangerfriends ~
Susan Ahlbrand

Alone in a full house
Still in a chaotic day
Haunted by the tickle of thought . . .
I become inspired by
a challenge
a mentor
an inspiration

by a strangerfriend

I put aside the needy students
I steal attention away from a house full of kids
I ignore my husband of 25 years
to prod my brain, my heart, my memories
for a creation in response.

Oddly, I open up to a room of strangers
sharing thoughts and feelings
that I wouldn't share here in the home
where I am sheltered in place.

I am awed by the vulnerability others show
the raw sharing of abuse
the honest telling of fears
the open storytelling
the beautiful describing

with strangerfriends

I've often been skeptical of stories
of people finding "friends" online . . .
gaming, discussion boards, tinder.

Not anymore.

The safe culture
cultivating creativity and sharing
the honest, positive, specific feedback
affirming
encouraging
complimenting

from strangerfriends
in these uncertain times
full of anxiety and instability
void of connection and activity
the one constant has been
#verselove.

bringing comfort and wisdom
and inspiration and confidence
this room has been
cozier than being huddled up
under a fuzzy blanket on a couch.

I will forever be grateful
for the Godsend

of strangerfriends.

One Morning ~
Susan Ahlbrand

I woke up one morning
about six weeks in and,
as in all things, the newness had worn off.

the fear and uncertainty of the stay-at-home order
usurped by complacence and comfort.

the scattered, unsettled feelings of teaching remotely
replaced by confidence and routine.

the frustration of staring at a screen
offset by the absence of disruptive students.

the wistful longing for evening activities
overrun by the appreciation of home being the default.

Right now,
my life is not in danger
neither are the lives of any of my loved ones.
Right now,
my job is not in peril,
nor are the jobs of any of my loved ones.

So, it's easy for me
to concern myself with my daily rhythm.

Our "new normal," our new rhythm
shines a light on many things we were
missing out on that we didn't even realize . . .
family time at home with board games
and euchre and family movie night.
More home-prepared meals than in the last three years combined.
Arts and crafts and yardwork.
Books and podcasts and exercise
Daily mass online and regular time for prayer.
Yoga and time for soul-searching.

The days will never be long enough again
to fit all of the things that I now know I love
There won't be enough hours
to squeeze in the few chapters,
the walk and podcast,
the meal prep and clean up
bookending a meal that holds lively conversation
after a full day of work.

How can we return to our "normal" jobs,
our "normal" rhythm,
our "normal" evenings
when we found so much now
that we want to keep?

And then there's this . . .
I'm writing about my "new normal"
while others toil in dangerous hospitals
and work in understaffed nursing homes
and mourn the loss of loved ones.

I feel petty and superficial to worry about
what I want my days to hold.

Because, like all things,
the newness will wear off.

Living Is Better Than Dying ~
Susan Ahlbrand

Living in a house with a first-year teacher
helping her navigate unfamiliar waters
with a boat that just changed to a paddleboard

Living in a house with a 25-year veteran math teacher
whose nickname is Graber
"How do you do this?
"I don't want to do that."

Living in a house with a high school sophomore
whose first varsity baseball season got benched
his socialization has been stripped.
Learning from a computer has never been his thing.

Living in a house with a college freshman
who got yanked back home mid-way through
carving out and embracing his independence.

Living in a house with a college junior
who turned 21 in quarantine with no bars to go to
nowhere to flash that ID

Living in a house of Collective Discomfort
we can't worry about me in a time of we.
Together the six of us navigate newness
knowing that . . .

Living in a house
is better than dying alone
because Covid locked out
loved ones.

A teacher mom might say
(during COVID 19 shutdown) ~
Susan Ahlbrand

Things I did so naturally
a few days ago
make me take pause . . .

touching my nose, my mouth, my eyes.
turning doorknobs,
pushing/pulling doors open in public places
walking through a store grabbing whatever I wanted

Now it's needs not wants that are the focus
and even needs can't impose their will.

As cheated as we feel about missed experiences,
As confined as we feel about being encouraged to hunker down at home,
At the root of those emotions and the fear that hangs over them like a drape,
we know these changes are vital.
Or, at least with each passing hour,
we are sobered by reality.

We needed to slow down
We needed to quit cramming our calendars with activities
We needed to stop pushing our students to learn more, more, more
and to move beyond things they were developmentally prepared for.
We needed to bring God, Faith, church, community, fellowship, concern for others
back into the center of self.
We needed to be reminded that home is a haven,
that we don't need to go, go, go all the time.
We needed to cherish our country and our wondrous sites
and not constantly yearn to travel abroad

I hope to never again take for granted
hugging my loved ones
shaking hands at the sign of peace
dipping my finger into the holy water font
perching in bleachers watching high school kids compete their asses off
welcoming my son home after baseball practice
following my favorite teams on ESPN

browsing through a store picking up wanted items
standing in front of a class of captive yet captivated students

Seasons have been cancelled
Graduations
Weddings
Funerals
First Communions
Retreats
Birthday parties
Family vacations

All of the things that
reflect our freedoms,
show our love
celebrate our achievements.

Our circles have shrunk
and will continue to shrink
like Laura Ingalls
in a cabin the woods
just family
and self
and thoughts

We have to embrace
this drastic shift
play board games
play cards
read books
watch movies
enjoy homecooking
knit
cross-stitch
work jigsaw puzzles

In a time of social distancing,
we have the chance to connect
to grow more intimate.

Oh, the irony . . .
distancing draws us closer.

Ugly Feet ~
Gayle Sands

I hail from a family of tiny women with tiny feet—
Size five feet are "cute".
(Size five shoes look silly;
take no room at all.)
Huh!

I am not tiny.
My size nine narrows
are definitely
Not.
Cute.

My feet define ugly—
Really. Look up ugly in the dictionary.
My foot picture is there.
Long-boned, purple-veined.
Toes bent in all the wrong places
Toe-knuckles fighting their way toward the tops of my shoes.
Toe nails not worthy of polish.

My little piggies stay home because they are embarrassed.

These feet belong on a prehistoric beast,
(Thankfully extinct.)

My husband says
That if he'd met my feet first
He wouldn't have asked me out.

Truth hurts
Ugly feet

Dear Fifteen ~
Gayle Sands

Sit down, sweetheart.
You are not going to BELIEVE
    the things I have to tell you!
I am going to just sum it all up—
You are going to make more mistakes
    than you can even imagine.
But those mistakes are going to turn you into a very interesting senior citizen.

You will cuss. A lot. Probably more than you should.

Those plans you have?? HA!!!
Plans are made to be changed.

It will take three colleges to get your BA in a major you won't use and date
a much older man and find out that's no good and grow up and move away
and have a good job you hate and meet a guy that your mom hates and marry
him and have one child and then twins (not a smart move, by the way) and,
oh, yes—there's a recession that messes everything up and you get around to
teaching at forty and you finally have a job you love and then your kids will
grow up and move out. You will be a very bad housekeeper.

And all of this required a lot of cussing.
Even before 2020.
 (We won't even talk about that—you wouldn't believe me, anyway.)

So here is my advice, fifteen. Take it step by step.
Every decision and every mistake you make will teach you a lesson.
Learn from them.
Mix it up.
Make a different mistake every time.
(You were really good at the mistake thing in the seventies.)
Throw in a few good decisions now and again
just to keep it interesting.
(That guy your mom hated is a keeper, by the way.)
Love your people, get a lot of pets, and keep your weight down.
Your knees will thank you.

And a couple of cuss words will always clear the air.

You have a heck of a ride ahead, fifteen…

Still Some Work to Do ~
Gayle Sands

I remember the time
One summer...
A student rode up on his bike as I worked in the yard
He was dishevelled, grimy, jeans shorts and too-small t-shirt,
a grin wreathing his face.
He threw his arms around me in a sweaty hug.
"Hey, Miss Sands! How's it goin'? You're not going to believe this—
I'm reading a chapter book!"

And I was. My heart swelled just a little bit.
He had been almost illiterate, a seventh grader
at the alternative school where I taught.

I remember the time...

I thought that If we had accomplished this breakthrough,
Anything was possible. This was the reward we all seek.
I told him how proud I was.
We chatted about the book for a moment, then
      he looked over his shoulder, hopped on the bike, and,
         calling out, "See you later!", rocketed down the road.
 I chuckled and shook my head. Exactly what I was used to from him.

Two middle schoolers ran up, panting
"Did you see him? Which way did he go?
That's my bike—he stole it!"

I remember the time...
I realized that there was still some work to do...

Hugs ~
Gayle Sands

The last day of school was stolen from us.
No sigh of relief, no wave to the bus.
I couldn't hug them.

I taught from afar, a world in between.
No real connection, naught but a screen.
I couldn't hug them.

No farewell ceremony to close with.
Worse for them than for me, I suppose, but
I didn't hug them.

They are gone to high school;
 all the months we spent
dissolved, so many lessons unsent.
I can't hug them goodbye.

Hunkered in our houses, away from those we know.
Scurrying through stores, get in, get food, then GO!
If I see a friend, I wave, because
I shouldn't hug them.

My friends stay in touch with emails and such.
Better than nothing, but I so need their touch.
I want to hug them.
My daughter lives two hours away.
Our phone conversations happen every day, but
I haven't hugged her.

I talk to Mom on the phone every week.
As her mind fades, it's my presence she seeks, yet
I can't hug her.

On a walk in town, a student appeared.
"I've missed you", she cried, arms out, running near
I set aside my fear...

And I hugged her.

Origins ~
Gayle Sands

I was born
From Dick, Jane and Sally
in perfectly pressed clothes,
with clean blonde faces,
obedient dogs,
fluffy cats.
Look! Look, look, look!
Oh, how I looked.
I learned the power of the alphabet from Dick and Jane.

The Borrowers were my comforters.
Arriety, Pod, Homily, and Hendrearry Clock.
Even their names were borrowed, not quite right.
When I lost something,
I knew that they repurposed it in their Under-clock home.
The thimble a coffee cup, the spool a bedside table.
The loss stung less, then.
I learned to say goodbye to things without regret.

Golden Book Encyclopedias were my intellect.
Multi-volumed, shiny, primary-hued covers.
A-Ar, W-Z. Faithful friends.
They never threatened, always informed.
The covers lost their shine with overuse
The coating peeled off like sunburned skin.
I made sure to put them back on the shelf in order
So that I could pull the right volume out when needed.
I learned the power that knowing things offers.

My mother's Nancy Drew books
fueled my dreams of adventure.
Oh, how I wanted to be Nancy,
Multi-talented, skillfully shifting gears in her little blue roadster
(What does she drive in today's renditions?)
As she careened down the mountain,
brakes failing.

I'll bet she didn't even break a sweat.
And she was always right.
She was superwoman. She could do anything.
Nancy taught me to use my mind,
that risks were worth taking.

My grandmother's Gene Stratton Porter books
took me to the Indiana swamps—
Freckles, Girl of the Limberlost, Laddie.
Lives in 1910 were so simple, so hard.
Survival was at a premium;
Nature's beauty and savagery lay just outside your door.
I learned gratitude from Gene Stratton Porter.

I was born from words.
Sentences and paragraphs built me from within
Poetry, biography, adventure, mystery, romance
drew me out into other worlds.
I live there still.

Crier ~
Stefani Boutelier

I was never a crier
But my heart keeps breaking
Quarantined from truth
The marginalized
The oppressed
Opportunity spectrum
The gap is widening

I will not cry

Kids whose safety was in the four walls
Of our classrooms
Food
Insecurities
Health
Instabilities

Don't cry

Trolls
Hatred
Bipartisanism
Petty
Disbelief

I cannot believe it

Unemployment
Stimulus
Terminally ill
Last goodbyes
Via facetime

Hold it in

Try not to take it personal
The constant hate
Disregard for humanity
Dis-empathy
Distant from reality

I cry

Addicted Recovered ~
Stefani Boutelier

Smoking and polluting lungs
Hustling ganja on the corner
Sniffing snuff, stardust mind
Eyes glued to the dark web
Sipping each hour to gain freedom
Pills deadening the pain
Posting positives to public media
Ignoring signs and hiding feelings
Chomping, vomiting, overconsumed
Judging self through actions
Coping to ignore realities

Chewing gum and popping bubbles
Dancing through grass at a concert
Smelling snapdragons on a walk
Writing poetry for self or the masses
Sit-ups, push-ups, moving to gain
muscle
Meetings, meditating to awaken
Learning, connecting through virality
Talking through the emotional labor
Moderating motions through balance
Shaming self through guilt
Coping to understand possibilities

Mirror Mirror ~
London and Stefani Boutelier

MAN, I love dancing with my reflection
DOWNside is that it can be deceiving
UPSIDE is that I can make myself laugh, the
THE reflection doesn't show how I feel, the
SEE what I mean?
I can write flipped notes of secrecy
TIME is measured with every look
EACH mirror holds limitless possibilities

EACH mirror holds limitless possibilities
TIME is measured with every look
I can write flipped notes of secrecy
SEE what I mean?
THE reflection doesn't show how I feel, the
UPSIDE is that I can make myself laugh, the
DOWNside is that it can be deceiving
MAN, I love dancing with my reflection

*Originally published in Autumn 2020: *Fine Lines 29(3)*, 53.
*Golden shovel poem from "Reflection" and "Backward Bill" in Shel Silverstein's *A Light in the Attic*

Rhythmic Run ~
Stefani Boutelier

ready, set, run
earbuds, forte in my ear
legs in adagio
Ain't Nothin But a Gangsta Party
beats shuffle my arms forward
shoulders pop with caprice to a
Bidi Bidi, Zoom, or Waka

andante sways my core into cadence
Won't Back Down
humidity pulling my hydration out
Harder, Better, Faster, Stronger
the rhythm near my drums
builds a tempo in my stride
Blinding Lights
on the Otherside
an ensemble of emotions and goals

sweat with every roll of the heel
the longer I pace with the lyrics
the deeper my thoughts pitch away
from the mad, Mad World
escapism through a runner's high
even when my feet feel like
Titanium
   ...I Run the World

A Crowning in May ~
Jennifer Guyor-Jowett

I am a child,
one bead of a decade,
chosen for my knowledge
of memorized prayers
and early reading ability
of words and their sounds,
the shapes they make
falling easily from my mouth
yet untested before crowds.

I stand small,
surrounded by long-limbed children
tree trunk torsoed,
older by years
(seven if we're to count).

Light filters through,
a time lapse of
Virgin Mary Blue,
wings of angel gold
slanting across this prayer pilgrimage,
snapshots
projected on synapse screens,
the click, click, click
of the spent film roll slapping
against the spool,
each click
a flicker of memory.

I hold in place,
await my turn,
the voices before me
exact,
assured.

I know my Hail Mary
I am full of Grace
But the Lord is not with me
The words jumble
Blessed art thou
All eyes on me
Who art in Heaven
A prayer mix
Unhallowed be thy name.

My crowning crucified
in blood red words
and mortification nails,
the sour vinegar remains on my tongue
to this day.

{poem-ing} ~
Jennifer Guyor-Jowett

There is space between the stanzas,
a spilling of words.
Often, when I yearn to hear myself,
I wander between them,
draw breath from their souls.
I carry their glimmer in my hands.

Between two selves ~
Jennifer Guyor-Jowett

The first time I held my sons

o in
march
e five years later

the multitudes of the world

the cacophoning
sounds
the echoing
answers

reduced themselves to
just

the sanctuary
of

         two

an entire world

between us

every molecule and
atom

every heartbeat
drum-thrumming

        every solitary
        thread

of our
existence

held
together

        between two
        Selves.

Requiem Mass ~
Jennifer Guyor-Jowett

In this cathedral of our world,
we honor the dead.
The relentless waves have stilled,
a retreat on bended knee,
a threnody.
We no longer need their crashing beat.
The winds come to final rest,
harboring inside organ pipes
a lament.
We hear no more their measured breath.
The earth's hum has paused,
its ancient choir silenced,
an elegy.
Its voice sounds no more for us.
The fires doused and extinguished,
a dissipation of the dying,
a funereal hymn.
We heap all on its pyre.
Our voices chant.
Dies Irie
Echoes of the haunting.
Dies Irie
Our voices expand.
Dies Irie
Our own dirge.

"compassion it" ~
Maureen Ingram

compassion it.
My bumper sticker
implies and explains,
who I am,
what I try to do,
what I believe.
Each of us is hurting
in some way,
big or small.
Love deeply,
meet their eyes,
laugh together,
desire to love, and
to be loved.
Work hard,
with passion,
do justice,
seek to know,
be curious, and
wonder.
Travel widely,
and see,
how wrapped up in one another
we really are, and
really should be.
Take action,
even tiny steps,
fall on your face,
get up,
go again.
Give space,
reflect, and
write.
compassion it.

Magic Happens ~
Maureen Ingram

Poetic inspiration,
waiting
each morning,
for me to discover.
An enchanted stone,
glistening,
in the morning light,
for me to hold and rub and ponder
throughout the day.
I let my mind absorb the mystery of the invite,
fascinated, curious, mesmerized,
followed by
space
to wonder.
That's how magic happens.

April days floated by
alongside, inside, around, between, and about,
inspiration,
tapping something deep within,
stirring me,
nudging me,
stretching me
in new directions.
I have marveled at the journey,
nuggets and insight found,
surprising visits to time past,
traveling to the edge of places I still did not dare to go.
The charm of your comments
finding light and sparkle in my verse,
hidden messages revealed,
illuminating my writing,
welcoming.
That's how magic happens.

The glow and beauty of your poems,
your openness and revelations,
how they captivated and soothed,
appearing like angels,
letting me know you, as
loving, familiar spirits.
Your words
carried me to new worlds,
gave me courage to wander there, too, and
provided a glorious shelter-in-place.
A wonderland of poetry shared by you,
this community of teacher writers,
connecting me to you, you to me
creating a lustrous weaving of
written dreams.
That's how magic happens.

Today,
it is fitting that
there is nothing but grey skies
and so much rain,
tears from nature,
where I am.
I am in mourning
that this month has ended.
I'm on my own now.
Yet, I know,
that's never really true.
Future mornings,
I will find again
magic stones you left behind,
to hold and rub and ponder.
I will treasure.
That's how magic happens.

Are You Sleeping? ~
Maureen Ingram

Bug-eyed, wide-awake, 3:46 a.m.
I am thinking through our words
Again, and again, and again.

Why do I care so much?
Why do I wrestle like this?
Why do I feel so frustrated?
Why does it matter so much?
Why does it wake me up?

Bug-eyed, wide-awake, 3:46 a.m.
I am thinking through our words
Again, and again, and again.

If a child isn't learning,
don't we have to change
the way we look at it
the way we work at it
the way we are set up for it?

Bug-eyed, wide-awake, 3:46 a.m.
I am thinking through our words
Again, and again, and again.

We make plans.
We set goals.
We call meetings.
We offer prescribed supports.
We meet the letter of the law.

Bug-eyed, wide-awake, 3:46 a.m.
I am thinking through our words
Again, and again, and again.

We want the system to work,
the child to fit within,
rather than
bending,
turning,
stretching
to meet the child.

Bug-eyed, wide-awake, 3:46 a.m.
I am thinking through our words
Again, and again, and again.

I'm not sleeping.
Are you sleeping?

There's a Hand ~
Maureen Ingram

There's a hand sticking out of the closet,
Fingers curled, reaching, grasping,
The breath is faint, labored, forced,
What moves in the dark, thrashing?

There's a hand sticking out of the closet,
Which side of nightmare is worse –
Only a hint of what is emerging,
Or trapped within dark and cursed?

There's a hand sticking out of the closet,
A brave, fearless detective
She chooses to look within the dark,
To explore new perspective.

There's a hand sticking out of the closet,
Followed by giggles and pants
Just like Lucy in Narnia, she's
Determined to take the chance.

There's a hand sticking out of the closet
Breaking out, coming back to us,
Watch how isolation, dark, and scary
Meets daring and resilience.

There's a hand sticking out of the closet,
Freely choosing the unknown,
She knows deep and dark is also free
There is much magic at home.

Dad ~
Denise Krebs

sometimes symphonies
remain unfinished
a long, long time ago
he was 43 years old
the devil's only friend

the day the music died
he was singing
bye bye
too many kids to feed
too many emotions to weed
bye bye cigarettes
bye bye vodka

before they married
his widowed bride
was blind to
all the minor keys
in which he played
his childhood
a telling overture of the whole
rhythm and blues opera
what would an
abusive alcoholic's
magnum opus
be anyway
maybe it was the
seven kids lost in space
trying not to misstep
bad news on the doorstep

they turned out nice
not into vice
stayed out of jail
tried not to fail
cute at all costs
not too many lost
to dysfunction with alcohol

one
when promoted to chp captain
asked mom
watched him on the stage
hands clenched in fists of rage
do you think dad would be proud yet

Note from Denise about the poem: Stacey Joy's prompt was multiple-stepped but doable. I loved that. It was still my first week, and I wasn't too confident. This poem was healing for me. In addition, Stacey's prompt has inspired me to write other similar poems over the past months. (For instance, the Amaud Arbery poem for September's Quick Write.)

It's A Good Friday Just to Say ~
Denise Krebs

Incorporating William Carlos Williams' "This is Just to Say"
This week started with a parade I
Witnessed. Shouting and waving my palm branches have
Given me hope. Too often I've eaten
Of this desire, dreams for the
Future, broken again. Grapes and plums
Crushed into sour wine that
Is poured out and wasted. Were
You informed of this in
Heaven before you agreed to the
Plan? Heaven must have been an icebox
The moment the plan was devised and
Executed. Which
Brings us back to you
Here now getting lead-studded lashes. Were
You tempted to split the earth and let them fall in? Probably.
Crown of thorns, 'My-God'-groaning, but saving
Some bit of hope after the forsaking for
A fish-laden breakfast
On the beach. All to forgive
Us, the world, villains, sinners, trespassers, me.
Sour sponge dripping vinegar they
Gave to relieve your pounded nails, pounding head? Were
You aware that your godforsaken cries would become delicious
Victory over the grave, so
We would be able to say, 'It's Friday, but sweet
Sunday's coming,' and
Our scarlet sins could become so
Clean like fire and snowy cold

Note from Denise about the poem: This poem was written on Good Friday. I liked the way it just
rolled off my pen. It made me feel powerful.

Haiku ~
Denise Krebs

in these virus days
increased layers of litter
greet and expose us

Note from Denise about the poem: Day 18 - and Day 53 of the staying at home orders for me. I think it was about the time we started to all wear masks. Now it's been over 200 days, and we're still wearing and littering masks. It is a time of feeling exposed. The cases here are doubling and even close to tripling what they were earlier during the pandemic.

Four Things I'd Say to People Who Are Afraid of Their Spice Cabinet ~
Denise Krebs

1 – I used to be too, using cinnamon and basil and oregano and salt and pepper. When I felt exotic I'd add a pinch of cumin and a smidgen of chili powder. Nothing louder than what you'd find in a steaming bowl of chowder, though.

2 – Then I got older and bolder and experimented. I always loved to eat savory, flavory dishes, so why not recreate them in my kitchen? I can try. And try I do now because you see…

3 – My spices are becoming a touchstone for me. I look in my cupboard and see so many jars of hope, flavors brimming, ideas bubbling, whole leaves, pods, seeds, some crushed and powdered, as the hours are in my life. My time is limited in this place, in Bahrain where the flavors are exquisite and the spices are pennies. My time is limited on this earth. My time is limited in the kitchen, So,

4 – I want to use every hour, every recipe, every moment, every meal to the fullest. To the tastiest. To the joyful hope of a new beginning.

Note from Denise about the poem: The number 1 silver lining for me during this pandemic has been cooking. I was never much of a cook before. You asked us to write a spoken word poem. I wrote this that day: "When I saw your prompt today, I laughed aloud imagining for a moment what would have happened if this was a first day prompt. I would have run for the hills! Perhaps forever and a day climbing back under my "no poetry" rock. Thank you for waiting until Day 26! Today I felt it was a fun challenge instead of sending me packing."

Writing with #Verselove ~ Denise Krebs

Thank you, mentors
Thank God for writing
Writing poems
Writing hearts
Hearts of longing
Hearts of healing
Healing traumas
Healing brokenness
Brokenness once unspoken
Brokenness poured out in poetry
Poetry of triumph
Poetry of laughter
Laughter in knowing
Laughter in tears
Tears of renewal
Tears of cleansing
Cleaning from old hurts
Cleansing like therapy
Therapy of self-awareness
Therapy of celebration
Celebration of spoken words
Celebration of written words
Words like treasures
Words like flowers
Flowers of magic
Flowers of moods
Moods to relay
Moods to wander
Wander not aimlessly
Wander to ponder
Ponder hindrances
Ponder existence
Existence of whispers
Existence of universal truths
Truths to craft in form
Truths to craft freely

Freely speaking our hearts
Freely reading one another
Another day passed
Another poem written
Written in quiet
Written in embrace
Embrace our new friends
Embrace our sure future
Future of hope
Future of #verselove
#Verselove sustains
#Verselove restores
Restores
Sustains

And may I just add this poem I wrote earlier in the month. I still overuse my favorite superlatives, but your poems have touched me. I thank you for being a force in my growth this month. Many blessings to you all!

An Ode to #Verselove Poets
Wow!
Powerful!
Beautiful!
Lovely!

To my friends:
When I write these words it doesn't mean
I don't love your poems,
that I'm not truly touched.
I am.

To myself:
But come on, Denise,
that's all you write.
You are 62 years old.
Learn some precise language
for speaking about what you mean.
How about using a thesaurus?

Try...
striking
compelling
convincing
aced spelling

revealing
healing
appealing
got me dealing with my own feelings

reflecting
connecting
respecting
collecting
wisdom from you, my mentors

exposing
imposing
disclosing
composing that closing

With your words
my soul you're jabbing
my heart you're stabbing
my mind you're grabbing
my eyes I'm dabbing

Your poems are cathartic
for the arctic
sea in me
reminding me of open wounds
yet to be restored when
given your remedy

Note from Denise about the poem: Finally, I thought this Blitz poem said a lot about what had happened over the month for me about how important the community who had read my poems had become. It was healing and comforting during a difficult time to laugh and cry with these special people. It also is a shout-out to Glenda Funk who taught me about the Blitz back on Day 2, Glenda, who I met the month before during the Slice of Life blogging challenge and had encouraged my participation. (She still remains a faithful reader of my blog on the Tuesday Slice of LIfe stories challenge. What a gem she is!)

They Haven't Yet ~
Stacey Joy

They haven't yet heard their mamas wailin'
When their daddies got caged no chance for bailin'
"Don't understand, ain't done nothing wrong!"
But skin too black and mind too strong

They haven't yet gone to the Negro schools
Where white folks be callin' them nasty fools
Young church ladies try their hands at teachin'
On Sunday evening after pastors done preachin'

They haven't yet been beaten and kicked in the streets
But they seen hatred ridin' behind white sheets
White men breedin' their power and hate
In a country where nothin' ain't never been great

They haven't yet stood in line to vote
Rights and equality ain't even been wrote
Their own children haven't yet been born
In a nation where they'll forever be scorned

They haven't yet died while trying to live
They had only one smile and laugh to give
They had only one hand and hope to hold
They had only each other to love and behold.

The Golden Shovel Poem ~
Stacey Joy

What was life like BEFORE

This pandemic thought PUTTING

Us in isolation might bring FORTH

Kindness? Are we to BLAME

Can we ACKNOWLEDGE

Or consider THAT

Our collective hatred and ABUSE

Would have consequences? God DOESN'T

Like ugly, people ALWAYS

Say. But what may COME

FROM

Our solitude and shelter is AN

Embracing and gratitude of the beauty OUTSIDE

An unquenchable desire to discover our SOURCE

Of peace and love. SOMETIMES

We need silence and stillness. WE

ABUSE

Others beyond repair but we abuse OURSELVES

To God's despair. Go inward and examine yourself MENTALLY

Give your mind and soul an EMOTIONALLY

Uplifting message. Sing, dance and find a PHYSICALLY

Healing and strengthening practice. Rest assured, SPIRITUALLY

You are covered in God's grace and mercy. Use your isolation to FREE

YOURSELF

Free Writing ~
Stacey Joy

Writing without restraints
The freedom to go with my own ebb and flow
Knowing my words will land
In the safe spaces of your hands
Fearless and bold you say I am
But I still hide and seek myself, my story
Writing with you
Unleashes more of me
Showing me how to be proud
Unafraid to reveal a few cracks
Some big gaping holes
That I gently fill
One poem at a time

Grateful for my struggles
My obstacles and issues
My blessings and joy
They strengthen and sharpen me
Grateful for poetry, poets, and you!
"This is where
Floating rainbow hearts
Ascend to the ceiling"

Where I'm From ~
Stacey Joy

I'm from "Put your hands on your hips
And let your backbone slip!"
From my mother's strong legs and thick thighs
To wide smiles and dark brown eyes
I'm from four generations of freckles and moles
To "Stop combing your hair so much and maybe it'll grow."

I'm from Gloria and Jay
Both graduates of U.C.L.A.
I'm from playing school and wanting to teach
To walking on the sink to get things out of my reach
I'm from Are You My Mother?
To Are You There, God? It's Me Margaret
I'm from creating a hidden reading room in a linen closet
To card-table tents and Barbie campers

I'm from a big yellow house on a hill in "The Dons"
To pool parties and Slip 'n Slide scratched knees
From backyard baby showers and Christmas Brunch
To classy Bridge players and domino dads talkin' trash
I'm from Hopscotch and laggers on the side of the house
To a daring first kiss that made me shiver and spit

I'm from Nestle Quik's chocolate bubbles floating in my milk
To Gogo Burgers and Tito's Tacos with guacamole
From burnt cheese toast and El Patio Mexican restaurant
To sardines and crackers after Saturday morning waffles
I'm from Nana's Monday night Russian Bank and Pokeno
To Mommie's badminton matches on Sunday mornings in the gym

I'm from "Drive safely and don't stay out too late"
To cheerleading at Friday night football games and Shakeys after
From "You will not be driving for 2 more weeks"
To senior prom and graduation parties past curfew
I'm from "Mommie, I think I'm pregnant"
To sedation at a clinic plagued with regrets

I'm from growing up and moving out
To dorms, apartments and owning my condo
From married with two children and too many jobs too young
To divorced, grateful, and balanced
I'm from the suffering of my mother's and father's cancer
To the resurrection of hope and joy after grief

I'm from struggle, suffering, injustice, and inequalities
To taking a stand, sitting in, and marching onward
I'm from knowing my ancestors had it harder than us
To trusting that God is still the same today and always
I'm from poetry, chalk, protests, and music
I'm from breath and spirit
I'm from love.

BLACK HAIR LEGACY ~
Melissa Ali

AFRICAN LEGACY
Regal
Crown
Glory
Dreadlocked
Braided
Twisted
Dhuku
Gele
Hijab
AMERICAN LEGACY
Covered
Scarfed
Burned
Permed
Hatted
Wigged
Weaved
Altered
Always a source of contention
Bald headed
Nappy headed
Chicken headed
Snap back
Peasy
All over the place
Looking like straw
Looking like you been in a fight
Looking a hot mess

LEGACY
The 1960's changed the narrative for many
Afros
Blowouts
Cornrows
Braids

Dreadlocks
Twists
Naturals
MY HAIR LEGACY
Both my grandmothers
Maternal and paternal were biracial
Not because their mothers were in love with white men
But because Black women are always the collateral damage of American
society
Both wore their hair natural
Long
Wavey
Thick
What is known as "Good Hair"
Both my grandmothers said they married the darkest man they could find
so they could have
"Brown nappy headed babies"
My mother's hair
The opposite of her mother's
Short
Crunchy
Thin
But most of the time it was natural
And how I love her sandy, pink sponge roller laden hair
It was the late 80's when I became conscious,
Or what is now called WOKE
One part, foundation (that is how I was raised)
Another part, Afros classes in college
But mostly becoming the mother of a chocolaty, curly haired baby girl.
A baby girl that needed to see her reflection not only in my eyes,
But also in my appearance.
So I excised the colonizer's deeply rooted indoctrination that blonde straight
hair is the golden standard of beauty.
GONE are the blonde highlights I'd worn in my hair since high school
Tryin' to look like Miss Clairol
Gone is the over processed burnt up lifeless hair
Tryin' to look like Gwyneth Paltrow
Gone was the mindset that my hair needed to be tamed, controlled, and
seasoned

Like an enslaved African in the 1600.
My hair
My crown
My glory
Big
Puffy
Coiled
Tangled
Wild
My daughters, now two
Their hair
Their crowns
Their glory
Devoid of chemicals, heat, weaves and dyes
Full of self love,
Hair love
Woke
A new
BLACK HAIR LEGACY

Daughter of ~
Melissa Ali

My name is Child
I am the great-granddaughter of Celestina,
Mamá,
Miss Celeste
Who was a survivor and an epic matriarch
Obeah woman blood
Mamá refused to be the white men's collateral damage
Having to continue to work for her rapist, she gave her baby his last name
Always referring to him as "Dat white Bastard"
Her fingers spoon fed me castor oil
Her accent thick only knowing Spanish and Spanglish
But what she did best was cursed as the soles of her slippers
That she threw across the room and upside your head with accuracy
She taught me to mind my own damn business

My name is Little Girl
I am the granddaughter of Esmeralda Victoria
Essie
Miss Essie
Mamácita
Who was a survivor and a bad-ass matriarch
Blood stained hands
A Garvey-ite
Third world, poor, with eight children
There was nothing she couldn't do
Cook, bake, sew, garden, crochet, hustle
Mother to everyone in need of love for 102 years
But what she did best was feed the souls of the hungry
She taught me that family is not made of blood alone

My name is Missy
I am the daughter of Ida Celestina
Mother/Ma/Mommy
Mrs. Porter
Auntie Ida
Nani
She is a survivor and compassionate matriarch

The blood of Panama, Black Nurses, Black Power, and white distain
Violated, battered, and hopeless
She rose like a phoenix from the ashes
BSN-MFCC
Like her mother before her, opened her heart and doors to all
But what she does best is inspire others, and laugh
She taught me how to feel authenticity.

My name is Melissa
I am niece, cousin, sistah, community daughter, and auntie
Gurrrrl
Cousin
Auntie Missy
Melissa Ann
We are survivors and family
Some blood some not
Cooking, eating, drinking, laughing
Consoling, crying, cussin, and caring
All woven into the tapestry that is one
Ride or Die, bring a gun to a knife fight
But what we do best is be present for one another
They taught me how to love and accept the people you call family

My name is also Sister Ali
I am the daughter of revolutionary matriarchs
Harriet Tubman
Ida B, Wells
Toni Morrison
Dr. Francis Crest Welsing
We are survivors and kindred spirits
Blood in blood out
Fighting, writing, living, and breathing for the betterment of our people
Heavy hearted, laborious, and traumatizing work
God's warriors, working from the soul
Ripping off the bandages so we can heal
But what we do best is live in the truth
They taught me one voice, one action, one heart can become a movement

My name is Melissa Ali

Desensitized ~
Melissa Ali

The last time I cried for a Black person shot by the police was when 12-year-old Tamir Rice was killed by Officer Loehmann in 2014 for playing in the park.

The last time I felt rage for a Black person shot by the police was when 23-year-old Korryn Gaines was killed and her five-year-old son Kodi was shot by Officer Royce Ruby over a traffic warrant.

The last time I felt pain permeate my soul for a Black person shot by the police was when I watched Officer Yanez's bullets penetrate Philandro Castile, fatally shooting him during a traffic stop in front of his fiancée Diamond, her four-year-old daughter, and Facebook live.

The last time I felt disgust about the death of a Black person under the remand of the police was when 28-year-old Sandra Bland allegedly hanged herself in a jail cell with no physical evidence (finger prints, method, or video surveillance) that proved suicide.

From 2015 to 2020, 5,000 Black men, women, and children have been killed because of implicit bias, racism, fear, and anti-Blackness that is pervasive in the policing of this nation.

Numbness flows through my veins with the coldness of the Antarctic Ocean.
Heart broken,
unable to grieve,
desensitized,
and traumatized.
I can only manage to study these deaths with the eyes of an analyst.
I can tell you the exact moment George Floyd took his last breath.
I can give you a minute by minute recall from the time Breonna Taylor was killed until they removed her from her home.
I can tell you why it took 74 days for the police to arrest the murders of Ahmaud Arbery.

But what I cannot do is shed a tear,
feel any pain,
or muster up any anger for the unjustified deaths.
I am numb.
I AM SO NUMB,
That I too
Can't breathe.

Dance Party Fun ~
Tamara Belko

We dance with no technique
purely wild abandon,
there's really no mystique,
head-banging, body rockin,
chasing a mad shimmy
across the kitchen floor
Alexa belting music from … the 80's?
No worries,
my kids can groove
raised on a variety of smashing tunes —
Rock n roll, alternative, and musicals swoons.
We can dance and sing
"Mama Mia" & "Bohemian Rhapsody"
Without pause, quite amazing actually
We dip and skip and sash shay away
push those blues to another day
Without a doubt, we are crazy family.

Listen for your Beat ~
Tamara Belko

Verse one
Sweet lullaby
whispered in soft alto
A caress on your baby cheek
Listen for your beat
Verse two
Jubilant two step rhythm
Splashing in puddles,
Bounding down streets
Playing in allegro
Listen for your beat
Verse three
When you feel disconnected
and dissonance bellows
I will always be your counterpoint
Listen for your beat
Verse four
Let me soothe your worries
In a sweet cadence
When the world sees you as an
interlude, off pitch, staccato …
I will always love your vibrato
Keep listening for your beat

To My Dearest Daughter ~
Tamara Belko

College online means indulging in
homemade lasagna every day if you'd like,
no skimping on the mozzarella cheese, baby!
and there's copious amounts of red wine, the kind you
can't afford at school, not
that I'm encouraging excessive drinking, but still …
It's more satisfying to drink with family
Remember, this too shall pass
No, you aren't in Kansas anymore, but
pancakes taste better with chocolate chips, you're
welcome, there's a can of whipped cream in the fridge,
no judgement here
Look on the brightside,
there's a gassed car in the garage and
the keys are right where you left them
Never fear, where ever you go, that's where you are,
because there's no place like home.

How to Come Undone During Covid 19 ~
Tamara Belko

1. It begins with a steamy mid morning shower, scalding my skin, standing in swelling water ankle deep. I curse the clogged drain and stagnant water.

2. Organize my shoes, organize my sweaters (which I'll need until June), organize my sock drawer. Maybe I'll find the lost ones.

3. Wash my hands, stare at the bleeding fissures. Repeat.

4. Listen to 90's Grunge music from dead composers on repeat. Yeah, "I got a real complaint."

5. Pull the thread on my sweater.

6. Obsessively check my email for a response about manuscript submission. Think, "Is there anybody out there?" Check query tracker, check submittable. Check my email again. Convince myself I'm not a complete failure.

7. Use the app on my phone to track the dead.

8. Plunge shower drain, yank out strands and strands and strands of hair. Curse. It is all mine. I'm sure of it. What's worse than isolation? Going bald during isolation.

9. Wash my hands, stare at bleeding fissures. Repeat.

10. End the day with a heavy glass of red wine. Watch bleeding fissures. Count the dead. Pull the thread. Make a note to call the plumber.

Now What? ~
Kate Currie

What's next?
Always moving
Obsessed with progress
Agonizing over next steps
Never relaxing
Fearing stagnation.

Slowly,
Stress,
Snowballs.

Stop.

Breathe.

Enjoy the moment.
Enjoy the students.
Enjoy the work.

Mom, I cant spell it ~
Kate Currie

Even when I try!
Really, its too long
Can you spell it again?
M-E-R-C-E-D-E-S

Every day, I practice
Dyslexia wont sever the link.
Each time it gets easier
Slowly, I cement the link.

***

A name that is a the link
Between a grandmother
and granddaughter
that share
a passion
for education,
a love
for music,
an enthusiasm
for hard work.
One is here
and one is passed
But the name connects us
beyond the divide.

The Most Good ~
Kate Currie

Do the most good
everyday.
Do the most good
even if it is small.
Do the most good
even if you're alone.
Do the most good
when you feel strong.
Do the most good
when you feel lost.
Do the most good
despite the pressures.
Do the most good
despite the stares.
Do the most good
because you can.
Do the most good
because if not you,
then who?

It Embraces Me ~
Monica Schwafaty

Here is the place that reminds me that it is time to get to work
whether it is beautiful or gloomy outside
whether I feel tired or energized
A small desk with a comfy chair, my office
A computer sits on top
Waiting for me to start
It has become one with the desk

It is a simple desk, nothing fancy
But it is much nicer than the one in my classroom
It welcomes me every day
I spend more time here now than anywhere else
It never gets sick of me
And maybe I should hate it
But I don't
it sits facing the ocean
what else could I ask for

This desk, my office, has become my classroom
it welcomes my students, my kids
it's where we laugh and keep the bond alive
it's where I realize how much I miss them
it's where we go on a tangent and engage in deep discussions
it's where my kids amaze me

It is an unassuming desk, and it looks cold and distant
That's misleading, though
It has become my haven
It's where I'm becoming a writer again, after so many years
of holding it in
the words storm out
This desk
It embraces my inner feelings, dreams, and desires, and
It keeps them safe until I'm ready.

Ritual ~
Monica Schwafaty

Coffee in bed
Courtesy of my fiancé
"Quarantine is not so bad"
Reach for my phone
Facebook, Instagram
Twitter, the news, email
#Verselove
Read it
Dissect it
Self-doubt
"Maybe, I'll skip today"
Refocus
Read
Grateful for the early writers
Blown away by their talent
Brain at work

More coffee
Yoga time
What a treat
One may think I've forgotten
But that is not the case
My brain is at work
Yoga feels great
I feel more capable now
Energized, I get ready
Brain secretly at work

More coffee
Time to work
I turn on my computer
Grades
Google Classroom
Google Meet
Maybe today will go better
Teach

Break
Teach
Break
Teach
Break
Today is not better
Sick of virtual teaching
Parents
Students
It's never-ending
Brain still secretly at work
Last cup of coffee
I'm exasperated

Empty cup
My brain reminds me
I need my refuge
I need my haven
I need my escape
I'm ready

Sipping hot tea
I start typing

Anxiety ~
Monica Schwafaty

Anxiety creeps in
An incessant cough takes over
It'll be a mess
I'm not prepared
How do I use Google Meet again?
What if a student acts out?
How many will show up
Does that mean
I'm a bad teacher
Urgh…I miss being in the classroom
This is not teaching
I miss the connection
When is this going to be over?!

It wasn't so bad
It was actually quite fun
Google Meet, I love you
I loved "seeing" MY kids
The connection is back
We are a "family"
Some were quiet
Others were cheerful
Some were sleepy
Others ready to make jokes
One had Rex, his guinea pig
Who knew? In 8th grade?
An unexpected guest
but simply adorable
Anxiety is gone
Cough is better
Excited for tomorrow

Why should you participate in the #verse love celebration? ~ Monica Schwafaty

ONE- Because even though your self-doubt makes you hesitate, later you'll be glad you did it.

TWO- Because you can. Because you want to. Because you love poetry. Because you NEED it.

THREE- Because as you share your writing, a loving and supportive group gently embraces you. Their comments help you gain the confidence you so desperately need. These fellow writers/poets make you feel safe enough to take risks. You finally let go of your fears.

FOUR- Because it gives you a purpose. You look forward to it every day, and it helps make the mundane daily tasks a little less boring. You cannot go to bed without writing your poem. No matter how tired you are. It becomes a daily ritual. It allows you to stop and breathe.

FIVE- Because it helps you see the world anew. It connects you to your own and everybody else's humanity. It reconnects you to the writer you left behind decades ago.

SIX- Because the poems become a source of comfort and normalcy in a time when absolutely nothing is normal. It becomes a much-needed outlet, a haven you didn't even know you needed.

SEVEN- Because it gives you an opportunity to look back. You share memories, revisit events, and realize things about yourself you did not even know or had forgotten. You share some of the poems with your loved ones and you bond even more.

EIGHT- Because as you share the experiences that have defined who you are, you find your voice.

Me ~
Monica Schwafaty

It haunts me
penetrating my soul
leaving me in anguish
making me feel hollow
longing...
Always there...
The first thing in my mind when I wake up
The last thing in my mind before I fall asleep
The one thing that wakes me up in the middle of the night
wanting to scream, to run away
I cannot escape it
It's around me, it's within me
It consumes me
It is me

Infection ~
Monica Schwafaty

Stay inside for my own protection
Stay safe in self-isolation
It's only been a month
No one talks about it
Because it isn't easy to admit
It's only been a month
Quarantine is a prison
It's a slow demolition
It's only been a month
It is happening everywhere
Does anyone care?
It's only been a month
There is no escape
How much more can I tolerate?
It's only been a month
Quarantine is meant to stop the spread
But it fills me with dread
It's only been a month
The abuse is an infection
flourishing in this condition
It's only been a month
How much longer can I endure?
For I see no cure
And it's only been a month!

The Chair Calls Your Name ~ Sarah J. Donovan

The chair calls your name to write again.
The blank page awaits. Sit. Begin.
Fingers speak stories, a writer's trance.
Ache. Radiate. Enough for today. Stand.
The blank page awaits. Sit. Begin.
Craft words from trauma, love, sin.
Ache. Radiate. Enough for today. Stand.
Nurture the body that held your hands.
Craft words from trauma, love, sin.
Move beings into spaces to face fears.
Nurture the body that held your hands.
Mountain. Bridge. Warrior. Child's.
Move beings into spaces to face fears.
Fingers speak stories, a writer's trance.
Mountain. Bridge. Warrior. Child's.
The chair calls your name to write again.

Community Organizers ~
Sarah J. Donovan

Where do the fireflies go
when the dark skies
extinguish stars,
when tyrannical winds
rattle mighty crowns
and branches reach
for the ground
to save their leaves?

Where do the fireflies go?

They speak the language of light
synchronizing flashes
to defend, to warn, to attract,
thriving where they were born
at the margins of ponds and streams
near standing water,
shallow depressions
in forests and fields.

Where do the fireflies go?

They're feasting on worms, grubs,
slugs, and snails,
immobilizing their prey
with toxic schemes
sucking out the entrails
to fortify their kin.

Where do the fireflies go?

They are planning a revolt to strike
down street lamps and porch lights that filter
their radiance, to shatter the glass jars that suffocate
their wings, to plant flowers full of pollen and nectar
to fill summer dusk with
synchronizing flashes of hope
when the winds subside.

Sands of Time ~
Sarah J. Donovan

city blocks and ramps of streets
lanes of paths welcome bare feet
and powder blankets for miles of heat
i look at sand that way
but now winter powders cover dredge
winds of cinder and ashes spread
so many things I would have said
but sand got in my way
i've walked the sands toward dreams
cut my toes on hidden glass schemes
it's sand's forgiveness that I seek
the hourglass of time, a rhythmic beat
and soft landings on an oceanfront beach

Where I'm From ~
Sarah J. Donovan

I am from wastebaskets
from Johnson & Johson's talcum and Comet scouring powders.
I am from the bedrooms of plywood and glue,
the bathroom of mildew and dripping faucets,
the dining room of picnic tables and benches
with scratches and knots of battles and laughter.
I am from the rose bush
with temperamental blooms.
The magnolia tree
whose teacup blossoms I remember
as if they were my own palms.
I'm from Cream of Wheat packets
for breakfast and
french toast out of the skillet
for dinner.
I am from Skippy and Corky
skulking late to Mass
and Mother's Day breakfast at McDonald's with placemats
and from vacuum hums in the middle of the night.
I am from "go to confession" and "help your sister"
and "Islands in the Stream."
I'm from Poppin' Fresh after concerts.
I'm from Chicago and Collodi,
lasagna and Steak-umms.
From Papa, taking on Capone's goons
immigrant, educated in shake-downs. and alleys.
From rosaries of wood and glass and wire
wrapped in fingers,
resting in drawers,
hung on nails
waiting for prayers.
I am from long arms, blue streams in wrists
that have harmed and hugged.
I am from
the branches that scratch and knot.
Palms up, fingers nimble
I am from
the blossoms that cradle hope.

Sun Through Window ~
Betsy Jones

view from my back porch
view from my kitchen window
window that frames green grass and tall pines
window that captures the remaining blooms of camellias, lilies, and azalea
azalea blossoms dried like deflated balloons
azalea blossoms in a makeship vase, a green cup
cup caked with flour and sourdough starter
cup in the sink, on the counter, by the bed
bed unmade (nothing new)
bed dark and cool, calling me to nap
nap on the couch (normally reserved for weekends or holidays)
nap denied (zoom meetings and google hangout classes)
classes for homebound students: misplaced modifiers, author's purpose
classes for this amatuer breadmaker and misplaced teacher
teacher-dreams of unfinished lessons and unruly students
teacher without a classroom (just a dining room table)
table set with nice dishes, repurposed for online instruction
table strewn with notebooks and to-do lists
lists of student essays to read
lists of house projects and cleaning priorities
priorities reframed, units and standards re-aligned
priorities reordered, time no longer measured in semesters or periods
periods of calm and peace and gratefulness
periods of worry and anxiety and panic
panic-baking: pear and goat cheese galette, tahini chocolate chip cookies,
yogurt flat bread
panic-cooking: shepherd's pie, spinach pesto lasagna, chicken enchiladas with
green sauce
sauce pans stacked high, cheese crusted on plates
sauce simmering on the stove, garlic and onions season the house
house-bound, relishing the long hours reading a book or sewing a blanket
house warming in the afternoon sun
sun casts shadows across the lawn, squirrels chitter in the trees
sun sets behind the neighbor's house, a pink glow
glow of porch lights line the street
trees stand guard in the night

The Golden Shovel ~
Betsy Jones

In the mystical moist night-air, and from time to time,
Look'd up in perfect silence at the stars.
–"When I Heard the Learn'd Astronomer," Walt Whitman (1867)

In the cloudless dusk
the International Space Station appears. A
mystical and perspicuous event. Eyes
moist with anticipation and allergies and awe. A deep inhale of
night-air, cells fill with oxygen, the act of respiration both a magical act
and a biological fact.
From a back porch in Nowhere, Georgia
time expands, and I occupy the same space as astronauts in orbit, connecting
to thousands of eyes that trace the same arch from southwest to northeast.
Time contracts as the twinkling dot moves swiftly and smoothly over my
roof line. As I
look'd up through the perfect space between the oaks and the pines,
up beyond the bats that pirouette and swoop, I follow the satellite until it
disappears
in the east, behind the Berhl's tennis court. I hold my breath, trying to hold
this
perfect moment for a few more seconds. The
silence broken by the shouts and yelps from the Pickleball game. A final
glance
at the yard as the darkness descends,
the blue gone from the sky. The evening's first
stars appear, the sentinels of explorers, sailors, and poets alike.

I am from ~
Betsy Jones

I am from Childcraft Books
from Bisquick and Dial soap
I am from the "other Georgia"
red clay, gnats, and cicadas
I am from sweet onions and lantana, peanuts and daylilies,
the citrusy floral perfume of tea olive trees
I'm from front porch swings and droopy eyelids
from Robert Edward Jones, Jr. and Traci Lynne Hutchison
I'm from the short-tempered and the story-tellers
from "dark thirty" and "sit up straight"
I'm from Advent wreaths,
silver and gold ornaments on the Chrismon Tree
from "all is calm, all is bright"
I'm from ~~Ocilla Vidalia Leesburg~~ Moultrie
(30 miles from anywhere else you'd rather be)
lacey cornbread, streak o' lean-streak o' fat
From my parents' first meeting
(new teacher orientation,
homophone icebreaker,
engagement ring hidden in a pocket)
The dress my grandmother wore--with a peplum!--
for her first Ray City date with "that Jones boy"
on the walls lining the upstairs hallway,
on the mantel above the fireplace,
on the ledges and shelves of my mama's kitchen
the faces of aunts and cousins, grandparents and uncles,
brothers and vacations and long-gone pets
I am from these crinkled eyes and round chins,
these posed and candid moments,
this love and legacy stored behind glass

Borrowed Lines ~
Betsy Jones

Say we never leave our house again
Say we continue to mask and sanitize and worry
Say we plan our shopping trips like conquering generals

Say the tightness in my chest isn't panic
but a respiratory infection
Say the dining room table remains my office,
no longer a place for
full plates and
empty glasses and
shared stories

Say we keep making bread and slow-simmered sauce
Say we take afternoon walks and drinks on the porch
Say we sleep in and take naps and stay up too late

Say we never move to Birmingham,
never fix your family's house
Say we forget our dreams of new lives
of old neighborhoods turned hip
of Venezuelan food trucks or Indian kabobs
of day drinking in Avondale
of winter mornings at the bookstore

Say we never meet our niece
Say we collect and share our milestones on Zoom and Facebook
Say we delay taking your dad to Greece (for yet another year)

Say we never watch a movie in a dark theater,
never watch a play or concert or comedy show
Say we never go back to the beach,
white sand and salt waves and sweaty beer cans gone
Say we watch the world end from our couch,
from the end of our bed
not with a bang but with a whimper

Say we never buy a house, never root this nomadic half-life
Say we never have kids, never adopt or foster
Say we spend the next decade and the next one after that, just us

Say, It doesn't matter. Say, That would be
enough. Say you'd still want this: us alive,
right here, feeling lucky.

Inspiration: "The Conditional" by Ada Limón, (the last stanza in italics are her words)
https://poets.org/poem/conditional

I am COVID ~
Susie Morice

I came on silent feet,
slipped underneath your door
lay lazy on the floor
waiting.
You soaped your hands,
mopped and scrubbed
it down the drain,
or so you thought
to stave the strain,
my novel presence there;
yet, weaseled in the corners
I scratched and clawed,
brazen, thirsting for a flaw, I hung
and ripped inside your lungs, infected,
knotted, left your song unsung,
finished you,
I slithered on.
In years to come
they'll mark my day
and build a wall,
carve all your names
on miles of marble,
a pall will fall
across the land,
a marker left:
the COVID Wall.

Cocktail Hour ~
Susie Morice

I need an elixir, a potion,
a witch's brew to get me through
2020 since lockdown started for me on March 15.

A salving cocktail, if you will,
could maybe numb the hurt
of 200,000 (and counting)
erased from the country;

a cocktail to salve the scary fears
my friends endured,
their fevers, coughing, pneumonias,
ventilators, quarantines
away from their loved ones;

a cocktail to assuage my teacher friends
at wit's end
on a rollercoaster of administrative indecision
"just teach online":
(virtual too euphemistic...far too benign),
no wait, in-person, no wait online, no wait, hybrid, no wait ...,
two full-time jobs
with parents at wits' end hammering
their email keyboards morning to night
demanding answers teachers don't have;

a cocktail that calms kids' confusion
while adults around them play out domestic drama,
voices muzzled, ignored
day after day;

a cocktail that hushes the deniers, those ill-informed,
head-up-their-a$$, anti-logic, anti-mask,
anti-sanity spewers, hoax-mongers of breathtaking ignorance;

a cocktail to set at my feet
where my beloved old Watty used to lie,
to get me through that silence;

a cocktail that grants me sleep.

As with the Shakespeare hags
with their cauldron brewing cocktail,
there go I:

"Round about the cauldron go;
In the poison'd entrails of potus I'd throw.
Toad, his henchman rudyominous, I'd pull from under cold stone,
Boil thou i' the charmed pot.

Double, double this toil's no trouble;
Fire 'em up and burn, let the cauldron bubble.

Fillet of fenny snake,
Toss in a pence, not worth a shilling, in cauldron boil and bake,
Eye of mitch and toe of frogsmillershill,
Rushian wool of jared and mal-onia tongue salivating swill,
Adder's fork barr no truth and blind-worm's sting,
Lizard's leggy kellycon and vulture's wing,
For a charm of powerful trouble,
Like a hell-broth boil 'em till they bubble.

Double, double this toil's no trouble;
Fire 'em up and burn, let the cauldron bubble."

The hangover would be worth it.

To Forget Never ~
Susie Morice

I remember ...
we held these truths to be self-evident,
matters of fact --
it was like this.
Certainty. Bold and bent with conviction,
declared, trusted that our house was built
with stones of exacting might,
treasured trusses of truth --
"I saw it with my own two eyes!
Counted with my own ten fingers!"
Our house shifted, suddenly sagged,
drafty, cleft in the corners,
window panes smeared
with a heavy impasto
of doubt,
a trompe l'oeil,
a sleight of hand,
rendering a different truth,
countering logic, papered in toxins,
dripping pathogens down the wavering walls.
Now when I remember --
the text in my left hand,
my other on my heart --
the mere act of recollection,
carries a new weight,
a sacred rite,
as if having been there,
as if bearing witness,
as if forgetting
promises the house will crumble.
I write to forget never.

2020 Duplex ~
Linda Mitchell

This poem brought all the wrong tools for the job
I've rolled up my sleeves to dig by hand

    2020 is a year to lend a hand
    gloved hands, smiles behind masks

Love thy neighbor is spelled w-e-a-r a m-a-s-k
After derecho, hurricane, flood, and fires

    Hurricane before flood, derecho before fires
    too many birds with nowhere to rest

Neither harvest-moon nor harvest time offer rest
There's a vote to bring in, cell phones to ring

    Approved counting is by tree trunk ring
    Closed eyes clasped hands circle the wreck

Poets throw lines to clear the wreck
This poem brought all the wrong tools for the job

Goals for Constitution Day ~
Linda Mitchell

Live up to my part of
　　We the People
Participate in building
　　a more perfect union
Insist peacefully on justice
　　even in and especially in protest
Contribute toward
　　national tranquility
Appreciate grave sacrifices made
　　for our *common defense*
Advocate for the well being of
　　our community, country
　　and whole world
Share *blessings of liberty*
　　with family, friends, neighbors
　　now and going forward
　　as someone of
The *United States of America*

Thank You Note ~
Linda Mitchell

Thanks for hands
that milked the goat
then made that milk
into soap
added rosemary
a hint of mint,
spoon of memory--
and friendship.

Praise for hands
that knit soft squares
made to wash away
dirt and wear.

Bless the feet
that delivered here
love-made gifts
with good cheer.

To close this note
I also thank
the goat for munching on
weeds and grass
from someone's lawn
for giving milk
as her part
in a summer swap
of poetical arts.

Sincerely,
Linda M. August 2020

Kindred ~
Linda Mitchell

She was a math and science Mom
I was built for pretty words

As we grew together
we fell in love by page turns

Her precision met my poetical
fairy tale by fairy tale
Bible story by Little Golden Book.

Terms of our peace laid out and agreed upon
from *Once Upon a Time* until *The End*.

Sun and Fun ~
Anna J. Small Roseboro

Today the sun shines bright and bold on all who head outside
Today we can't go out how we wish the sun would shine inside
Inside it would warm our friends longing to be out having fun
Inside, not free to travel; inside with no sun or strength to run
How I wish I could be of help to those who wish to be out
Out in the bright sun, feeling bold having fun
Fun because of full bellies poking out
Fun because they have the strength to run
But we won't give up we'll help where we can
But we won't give up whatever the time span
Span across days we remain sheltered inside
Span through weeks we'll keep our smiles

Is It Time to Go ~
Anna J. Small Roseboro

It is time to go. Time to move over so others can grow?
Show they have the passion that has kept me here so long.
Is it time to stay to accompany others on the way?
Will I know the time? Will I know the day?

To show they have the passion that has kept me here so long
They need space inside the place. Will I have the grace?
Will I know the time? Will I know the day
 To collect my stuff, step aside, or leave and go outside?

They need space inside the place
With space to develop their own ideas and so will I have the grace
To collect my stuff, step aside, leave and go outside?
Or will I stay right here and share in this glorious place.

They call me, "The Nudge" so they must not begrudge
The fact that I've left in a rush
Some day soon, with a smile they'll say as they blush
Now you can go your way. We are here to stay.
Thanks so much. We'll stay in touch.

We Need You! ~
Anna J. Small Roseboro

There you stand sexy and bright
Ready to bring me light when it's night.
Curvacious and zaftig, oh how you glow!
Crowned with a linen skirt, blanchy like snow.
Thin steel arms extend out stiffly.
A tiny button turns you on quickly.

What would I do without your beauty?
On dark nights, I could not do my duty
Sending out letters and sending out notes
Reminding my friends to research for their votes.

We've got to express ourselves on the ballot
We've got to see that life's more than a shallot.
We must peel back the layers and get to the core.
Learn the truth about government; there's so much more.

There you stand, firm and strong.
You've kept me company oh so long
Listening with me to many a song
While I'm stuck inside away from throng.

Shine on, my friend, keep bringing me light.
Push back the night; keep my smile bright.

Stymied by a Stylus ~
Anna J. Small Roseboro

I ordered a stylus online,
Blame it on COVID one nine.
I couldn't get out to the stores.
So I ordered, then went back to my chores.
I got what I ordered
But not what I wanted.

I thought I was so current communicating online, most of the time.
Now, as the devices are getting smaller and my fingers are getting stiffer,
I need help. The stylus is supposed to make me work swifter.
I just wanted one of those nobby nosed markers, not pointy like a cone,
To tap the letters and numbers on my tablet and cell phone.
Instead of moving forward with technology,
I'm having to go back to ancient times.
Nothing is really new. The oldies knew what to do.
Sharpen a stick and scratch out the letter.
Use the smooth end, to erase and make it better.

Everything old is new again.
The old fashioned stylus is taking a spin
And creating havoc for me!

I went online, thinking I'd get it time
I wanted to use I to draft this day's rhyme
To work really fast,
With something that will last
But it didn't work.
And It wasn't a quirk.
I just didn't know
My ignorance would show.
What goes around, comes around
I wish I'd known what I'd need for a phone.
Ignorance about an old fashioned tool
Is making this here lady look like a fool.
Now everyone knows, I'm not all that cool.

The Redwoods ~
Anna J. Small Roseboro

Walking through Redwoods Forest with my Honey,
Standing among the majestic giants is worth much more than money.

Who could imagine two hundred years ago
When the seeds that first fell down to the ground
The two hundred feet up these trees would grow.
The awesome breadth, thirty feet around!

The crinkly quiet as we walk around, listening for, but hearing no sound.
The twin trees leaning against each other remind us that we need each other
To stand tall, so we won't fall.
Like the Redwoods, we must stand fast to the last.

Oh God, we give You glory for it all.

Photo Credit: Joan Williams from Eureka, Ca.

Love It or Lighten It ~
Anna J. Small Roseboro

Love the skin you're in
Be satisfied and you'll win,
Unless your skin is black or brown
Then few folks even want you around.

"High yellow is mellow,"
Says the gawking fellow.
"And white is all right!"
"Don't even say it", I'll fight.

Melanin count predicted your life.
If you're dark, choose light for your wife.
Do so and lighten up the family tree.

Lighteners is what we were expected to be.
Those who purged the line of black
"If you're black," they said, "get back".

Thankfully, we were taught to be proud.
"I'm black and I'm proud!" we'd shout out loud
Today when I hear that exact same stuff
I turn a deaf ear and walk off in a huff.

Songs Soothe and Help Us Cruise ~
Anna J. Small Roseboro

Songs of praise help me get through the days
Hymns to Him remind me of ways
He helps get out, but not out and about
During forced days of inside stays.

Rhythm and blues when I hear the news
I reach for my running shoes.
Discordant news pulse within. I just want to jump and shout
Please just let me get up and get out.

Hallujujah's resound; so often out of tune.
While riding my indoor cycle, listening to YouTube, I croon.

Oh no! Another family member has died!
Not dirges this time; compassion accompanied me as I cried.
I rocked and swayed in my seat, reading another sympathy card.
"May melodies and memories remind you of our family's regard."
Folks may be dying all around, but flowers burst forth in the yard.

Jazz riffs in these poems, within the beat
Of the daily given challenge, be-bop along and are neat.
Each writer saying what's in the heart
Resolved to keep on living, giving each day a fresh new start.

Cheery notes from friends help us stay afloat
In these strident times, we're not alone in the boat.

Lead On! ~
Anna J. Small Roseboro

Sarah, congratulations to you.
With poetry, you've helped us to view
Our lives through another lens
And we now see ourselves as friends.

Congratulations to you, my dear.
We once were striving writers. It is you we cheer
You invited us to share your dream.
We're now a thriving poetry team.

I thank you from the depths of my heart
Because of you, I made a start
Created VERSING LIFE TOGETHER.
We'll keep writing despite the weather

We're learning to talk about life in rhyme
It's now more fun, but still lots of work.
Lead on, my friend, no need to shirk.
This work is worthy of your time.

A streetside elegy in C ~
Laura Langley

Our quintet gathers
on respective curbs
(More than six feet apart:
This distance is not mandated,
This distance is neighborly love,
This distance is
paradoxically
infuriatingly
against the status quo.
This distance is avant garde.)

Neighbors converse
Two octaves
cleaved together
cleaved apart
We are whole C notes
They are whole C notes
No notes between
We create dissonance
We create consonance

Once in a while
A car a cyclist a walker
Will interject an E or a G
A momentary
chord is struck
An interrupted cadence
head-nods smiles hello's

The Weather in 2020 ~
Laura Langley

On a scrap of paper in the archives is written
"I have forgotten my umbrella."
Turns out, in a pandemic everyone,
not just the philosopher, is without.
These days, I slather antibacterial gel on my angry,
red, cracked hands every time I get in my car--
I never even used to own antibacterial gel.
These days, I pull clumsily-fitting, homemade masks
across my face to protect
me
them
their families
my family.
Every slight ache, scratch at the back of my throat,
heated moment has me Googling, yet again, the symptoms.
When Rachel had it (all alone in Mexico City--just her
and an ornery, orange cat) she only lost her sense of taste,
8 days, but what next? Is there a sequel to this horror?
So I
buy clothes that can withstand virus-killing high heat,
buy shoes that never see the inside of my home,
join book clubs to discuss our nation's original sins,
buy more books than I have time to read to learn,
listen.
I pull the umbrella from under the backseat of my car,
So that I can meet my students at this moment.
A moment when the murder of yet another black man
in the name of law is a weekly occurrence.
A moment when leaders are living above the same laws
that keep so many in bondage.
And, also in this moment, I'm reminded that young folks
see and breathe truth. Young folks do not tolerate
what this country has passively accepted for 400 years.
We will get by. We will survive.

Note from Jamie about the poem: Inspired by Claudia Rankine's "Weather"

I draw my ink from ~
Laura Langley

another frustrating encounter with a student.
a disappointing conversation with a coworker.
an argument after dinner.

my intuition squaring up with my intellect.
the trembling, yet unwavering need for gloves-off bitching.
the pending therapy session.

beautiful words wherever and whenever they find me.
fleeting observations surely supercharged with meaning.
teaching by example.

Outcome ~
Laura Langley

I have a deep-rooted sense that
things
       will
       work
       out.

Of course they do: work out.

The universe grows itself.
The universe makes space for life.
The universe designs organisms for growth.

Like all living things,
we are microscopic   prototypes
of a benevolent universe.

I exist, therefore I am   good.

"Journey" ~
Laura Langley

I—we—journey through this well-worn, unknown
territory. Twenty down, twenty weeks
to go. Invisible change: bone,
organ, tissue, vessel. My low back creaks.
Cells install new plumbing that requires tweaks.
As it's evolving into its new form
I try to listen as my body speaks.
We prepare as if awaiting a storm;
contemplating the future keeps us warm.
Like packing for a months long trip at sea:
Gather stock, consult pros for the new norm.
Savoring the now while planning is key.
We charge on from one journey to the next
full of joy yet increasingly perplexed.

Looking for Signs in Spring ~
Barbara Edler

From here
Your favored spot
I watch
Elm tree buds
Frantically waving
I feel
Sun rays
Warming my face
I ponder
Pregnant clouds
Full of promise
I recall
Devil's Tower, last summer
An ominous wind's
Keening lament
I stared
At a burnt tree
Frozen in place
Were you calling to me then?
I've been waiting so long
For a sign
Today, gazing at the spring sky
In your favorite place
I wonder
Are you loved?
Are you safe?

Meltdown in Aisle Three ~
Barbara Edler

In Aisle Three
At Hy-Vee
I have a meltdown
Shelves literally wiped clean
No juice, no milk, no sardines
There's barely any meat
Except where the butchers work
I ask about an advertised sale on New York strips
I thought they had
They do, they're just not marked
I ask for four
The butcher looks relieved
Which makes sense later when
I discover from a friend someone had just come in and ordered
200 pounds of hamburger
I'm here for just a few items
And now I freeze
In Aisle Three
Tears forming the question,
What's yet to come?
My youngest son
was just married last week
Which never would have happened
This week
Knowing he works stocking stores
I fear he may get it
The thought of losing
One more child
Has me falling down
Gripping an empty shelf
So many plans are now on hold
The uncertainty of the future overwhelms me
As I pray for miracles
Amongst the cans of corn and beans

Rituals ~
Barbara Edler

Last year a knock on the door
Woke me from an uneasy slumber
Believing you were coming home
I never dreamt I would find
Two officers at my door
Eventually informing me
You were never coming home

Now I wake to a numbing weight
Daily exercising my best to bury it deep
Reminding myself to love
To forgive; to live with purpose
To believe you're in a better place
Carefully I straighten a homemade ornament
Cherishing it more than ever
Because at its center is
Your brilliant child's face

Now the day begins with
Wearing a necklace with your fingerprint
Dreaming of hearing your musical voice
Singing, "Oh, Mama Mia."
Imagining your warm embrace
Wishing I could have
Eradicated your demons
To have wrapped you so tightly with my love
That you would have never chosen to leave

So Much Depends on Covid-19 ~
Barbara Edler

So Much Depends on Covid-19
My son called today, so
Sad that his honeymoon was cancelled, much
Suffering lately; lives lost, special plans aborted, depends
On one's ability to love from a distance, upon
Lysol, gloves, protecting ourselves, each other, a
Cacophony of grief reverberates, red
As this ruined wheelbarrow

Note from Barbara about the poem: Inspired by William Carlos Williams "The Red Wheelbarrow"

From My Open Hand ~
Allison Berryhill

I give you
the benefit of the doubt
quick and generous laughter
rose tint on that glass
tilted toward the #IowaSky
a job that suits your skills
and leaves soft petals
as your footprints
I give you
gravel to run on
a new skill to learn
evidence of synergy:
a Broadway musical
a complex interstate cloverleaf
a four-leaf clover
the First Amendment
I give you
a chance to be kind (take it)
a chance to forget that slight (take it)
a chance to step up (take it)
a poem to write (write it)

Running from Both Sides ~
Allison Berryhill

Running
Pain and drain of energy
And weight of body's lethargy
The headwinds pounding westerly
I looked at runs that way

I've also run to hope and heal
To know the solace that is real
And afterward, endorphins feel
I welcome runs today

I've looked at running's cons and pros
Its ups and downs, its highs and lows
The motivation comes and goes
A twin-edged path this runner knows.

Note from Allison about the poem: Based on Joni Mitchell "Both Sides Now"

Ovillejo from the Earth ~
Allison Berryhill

I found upon the step a puppy's tooth.
I tell the truth.
Small and clean and white as milk,
Smooth as silk.
A treasure cradled in my palm,
A gift of calm.
Who knew a tooth as mid-day balm?
A small white star, come down to earth:
A tiny sigh, a tiny mirth.
I tell the truth smooth as silk a gift of calm

Note from Allison about the poem: Three rhyming couplets and a quatrain
"What has earth given you?"

Sonnet to VerseLove ~
Allison Berryhill

From April one to thirty, close of day
I wrote a verse according to the plan.
"Just do the verb to be the noun," they say–
I think, I think, I think, I think I can.

The Little Engine could, and so could I.
With fuel of gentle comments for my words
My willingness to share was magnified.
I chugged ahead because my thoughts were heard.

How can I recreate what happened here?
How can this vision turn into a plan?
How can I help my students face their fear?
My Little Engine chugs: "I think I can."
I think, I think, I think, therefore I am.
This Little Engine celebrates: iamb

Tense OverDue ~
Mo Daley

I'm afraid I'm losing my mind
I'm perpetually tense
Tense intense pretense
Tense every minute of the day
Day turns into night
Day one day two day three are all the same
Same stress
Same house
House is a place of work
House doesn't seem like home
Home is no longer cozy
Home is what I miss
Miss real work
Miss friends
Friends who listen
Friends who support
Support each other
Support our kids
Kids who don't understand
Kids who don't deserve isolation
Isolation that angers us
Isolation to save the human race
Race away from others
Race to the store
Store what we want
Store what we need
Need to walk away from technology
Need human contact
Contact old friends
Contact family
Family who I can't hug
Family so far away
Away from here but not my heart
Away from my embrace

Embrace the luxury to work from home
Embrace this time of reflection
Reflection sends my mind racing
Reflection on the important
Important things now change
Important people stay the same
Same thing day after day
Same heart being torn apart
Apart is painful
Apart is frustrating
Frustrating is something I can live with
Frustrating is a small price to pay
Pay the devil his due
Pay it forward with love
Love
Due

Night Terrors ~
Mo Daley

They come when I am happy
They come when I am anxious
They come when they will-
When I'm with a houseful of family celebrating in Colorado
When I've shared a delightful evening with my husband
When I've hiked Machu Picchu and am finally able to rest
The Night Terrors
They come without warning
Insidiously creeping into my psyche
Tugging at fears that are buried so far below the surface
That I didn't even know they were there
They prod, they poke, they push frantically
Until the bony hand of the man chasing me
Grabs me so tightly around the throat
That I can't scream
Although I am terrified,
I've never been one to keep quiet
So I try
And I try
And I try
To be heard
Until at last,
The low-pitched groan releases from my throat
Turning into a shrill, ear-splitting scream
That wakes the house
Welcoming them into my nightmare

Details of a Driveway Visit ~
Mo Daley

The blue painter's tape
running down the middle of the driveway
separates us.

So completely-

like mountains sprouted from seeds
like oceans born from salty tears
like walls fought for with hateful hearts.

But how can a child understand borders?

My Tiny Star ~
Mo Daley

Twenty years ago, the Star Magnolia was a mere bush in the yard when we
moved in
My boys were barely seven, ten, and twelve
They zoomed around the yard, throwing any and every kind of ball they
could find
The tiny Star Magnolia served as a hurdle for their running games,
Losing leaves when they jumped too soon.

We took family trips over spring break- D. C., Colorado, and California.
The fragrant Star Magnolia would bloom each spring whether we saw it or not.
But truth be told, I was always heartbroken when I saw the withered and
browned petals strewn about the lawn
When we pulled into the driveway after a vacation.

The boys grew.
Soon the Star Magnolia served as a backdrop for graduation and prom pictures,
Casting just enough shade on my growing giants.

The tiny Star has now grown to over twelve feet in height
And even my six-and-a-half-foot tall, little man can no longer jump it.
Since there was nowhere to go this spring,
I watched from the kitchen window as her petals fluttered and fell to the ground
But I thought of the new little boy, the son of my son,
Who will play in the Star's shade for so many years to come.

Fortunes for my sister ~
Emily Yamasaki

Fortunes for my sister, Dr. Tsai
Believe that this too shall pass.
Order in tonight, you deserve it.
Always add guacamole for extra charge – worth it.
Life is full of challenges, you got this.
You are an amazing doctor, but an even more amazing sister.
Don't worry, your patients can feel your kindness from just your eyes.
Be on the lookout for care packages.
May your coffee be as strong as your gown and mask today.
Never forget: you were born for this.
Self care. Do it. I don't mean yoga – I mean cookies.
You are a hero – and not just to me.

Abandoned ~
Emily Yamasaki

School Abandoned
No one sitting in those blue chairs
  Teachers care,
Dust on desks, no pencil tin
   it's really in
the dim, empty hall; no tracked mud
   our blood
feels lifeless without a "hey, bud"
A school with no pulse or heartbeat
eerie and just a bit too neat

Teachers care, it's really in our blood

The News ~
Emily Yamasaki

A global threat
is creeping within
unexpecting bodies
Taking one, two...
Two hundred thousand

But we are quarantined
But we are careful
But we wear masks
But we wash hands
Our home is our haven –

> *"We want to immediately share*
> *that one of our community members*
> *has tested positive for COVID-19..."*

No one is safe
How does one face
this fear?

Thin ~
Emily Yamasaki

This year I am
Stretched thin
Not the skinny girl thin
Nor the skim, might-as-well-be-water, milk thin
Not even the angel hair pasta kinda thin

The kind of
Stretched thin
Makes you wonder if nanny-ing would be easier
If fall 2020 is the one
Where you throw in the teacher towel

The kind of
Stretched thin
Makes you wanna
be
somewhere
someone
anyone
else

Chronic but Well ~
Katrina Morrison

Cystic fibrosis is a genetic disease
Cystic fibrosis is chronic
Chronic coughing is a common symptom
Chronic constipation is another
Another symptom is poor weight gain
Another symptom is a compromised immune system
System is altered on the cellular level
System degenerates over time
Over time medines have been developed
Over time procedures are improved
Improved lung function is always the goal
Improved school attendance is a result
Result of sputum culture determines treatment
Result of the x-ray can be pneumonia
Pneumonia is a bff - bad frequent friend
Pneumonia can mean a hospital stay
Stay away from anyone else with CF
Stay away from smokers
Smokers create second hand smoke
Smokers cause asthma attacks
Attacks are handled with nebulized albuterol
Attacks are prevented by nebulized saline
Saline cannot properly pass through the cell walls
Saline (a common salt) is present in sweat
Sweat tests can diagnose the presence of CF
Sweat of patients dries white on the skin
Skin can be affected by some medicines
Skin rashes like red man syndrome appear
Appear at the CF clinic on a regular basis
Appear at the gastroenterologist's office
Office at school must keep 504 on file
Office should understand nature of the disease
Disease delays growth and puberty
Disease results in high male infertility rates

Rate per capita is highest in Ireland
Rates are higher wherever the British colonized
Colonized in the lungs can be Staphylococcus aureus Haemophilus influenzae
Pseudomonas aeruginosa Burkholderia cepacia MRSA and more
More patience is required by patients who must spend
More time than imaginable on treatments
Treatments include performing respiratory physiotherapy
Treatments must occur multiple times a day
A day will include taking enzymes with every meal
A day may include using a Mic-Key button for nutrition
Nutrition must have an extremely high calorie count
Nutrition must have a high fat count as well
Well Staying well is the goal
Well in body mind and spirit
Spirit comes from the Latin word for to breathe
Spirit breathe spirit breathe spirit just breathe

Ekphrastic Poem ~
Katrina Morrison

It was the teacher's to assign
Who sat in each row and line.
Hung so proudly on display
Students work from yesterday.
Words and drawings illustrate
What the teacher would relate.
Teachers brought something to show.
Students came up row by row.

Cursive lost the writing race
Technology's now in its place.
Dressing up is not the style
We wear jeans once in a while.
Austerity we don't embrace.
We put up posters in its place.
Things have changed so very much
Are we any more in touch?

Golden Shovel Poem ~
Katrina Morrison

I'm able to enter unnoticed.
Nobody will know I was here.
Who needs all the air in the room.
Are not peace and quiet enough?
You will understand this, if you
Are at peace too.
You can't get enough of being
Nobody. You can't go
Too unnoticed.

Mirror Poem ~
Katrina Morrison

Commas precede
Conjunctions when
Listing items in
      A series.
        Oxford
      Rules!

      Never
        Place
        Commas
Before "and, but,
Or "or," when you
List items in a series.

Acrostic Analogy ~
Katrina Morrison

Stupefy is to stunning as
Protego is to protecting as
Expelliarmus is to disarming as
Lumos is to lighting as
Leviosa (Wingardium) is to levitating as
Scourgify is to cleaning.

Source: http://www.mtv.com/news/1914360/harry-potter-spell-ranked-by-usefulness/

Ovillejo ~
Katrina Morrison

Didn't expect to find you here,
Slithering near.

Your scales so smooth provide shielding,
Yet unyielding.

A single amber stripe I see,
Cautioning me.

As I kneel here on bended knee,
We're a terrestrial trinity,
Just earth, just you, it's just us three.
Slithering near yet unyielding cautioning me.

Distance Learning? ~
Seana Wright

Fifth
Students
Distance learning?
Are you learning?
Have technology?
Momma's cell or daddy's?
What is going on at home?
Who is there encouraging you?
Is there quiet and a place to write?
Will you be ready for middle school soon?

Brian Power ~
Seana Wright

Daddy was analytical
Mommy was emotional
He knew people
and she saw intention
They both could see BS
coming 'a mile away
They taught me to think first
and use your mouth second.
Didn't always do that
especially when I was
younger but time, being a teacher
and becoming a mother has
taught me
to "shut up" sometimes.
Daddy said to surround
yourself with like-minded people
those who are as smart or
smarter than you.
Mommy sat with those who laughed,
cried, analyzed, danced and cussed.
I enjoyed being the only child during my
younger years surrounded by scholars, educated fools
and souls in search of love and meaning.
I watch people now sometimes and wonder
why they're angry, ugly, thrilled or peaceful
What narrative is running through
their head and heart?
What narrative is running through mine?
I just want to make sure I stay
centered and always at peace.

Parent conversation- Code Switching ~ Seana Wright

"Mrs. Jones, Let's talk about your son Johnny"

Listen here lady, Ima 'bout to give you the skinny about your son. He's special.

"I'm concerned about his lack of attention during class"

You told me you took drugs years ago. Is he a drug baby?

"At times, he has difficulty listening long enough while I explain multiple-step math problems."

He listens five seconds then looks around for classmates to laugh with.

"He talks too much to classmates especially during individual work time."

I want to say "shut up and let them work, don't you notice they're quiet?"

"Yes, mom I can send some extra work home but that's not necessarily going to help."

You've got 3 kids younger than him. Worksheets aren't babysitters!

"I know you say he reads books at home and reads the dictionary daily but he doesn't do that here."

Stop lying. He's two grade levels behind and has been in reading intervention for 3 years.

"Your son needs more time and help so that's why I'm bringing up the subject of retention again."

Sign this paper right now so we can get your baby some help. You should've done this when the three previous teachers asked but you kept saying you'd work with him at home. You can't do that because you're not a teacher!!!

Writing Procedure ~
Seana Wright

Process
I read the topic
and the mentor text
I marvel at the samples and
wonder if I'm a fraud
then realize I'm not
I think of previous writings
I remember students, daughters,
friends, family, situations
I ponder how revealing to be.
Hurts, successes, events, strengthenings
ALL come into my brain
as I consider how much to confess.
All of this is done with a huge mug of
Kona Joe coffee and the quiet of a morning.

My Rectangular Honey ~
Seana Wright

I desired you before
I even met you.
You kept popping up
on commercials and
billboards begging me
to pick you and embrace you.
You appealed to my
sense of wanting to have the latest
gadget, wanting to be 'fly',
wanting to be a rockstar.
I forced myself, though, to wait a year
due to all the recalls and upgrades.
Once I had you, I slept with you, took you into the
bathroom, and downloaded a multitude of
unnecessary apps just so I could see
those colorful little squares.
Now that you're mine and we've been hitched for
10+ years, I still desire you.
You keep me connected to faraway descendants
you hold images of angels, my past and present,
and new learnings.
Also, though, you have brought me dreadful
words and have given me depressive
news that took me to the floor.
At times I'm addicted to you
like a 16-year old girl having the hots for a 20-year old boy
which is alarming considering
I lived without you for the first thirty years of my life.

April 29, 2020 ~
Margaret Simon

The day's date tops a crisp clean page.
A poem, a prompt, a quote muses me,
so I sip coffee and think on it
with a pen. Today's color is green.
Where does this poem want to go?
Keep the pen moving.
Magic can happen here.
Words can smooth out the wrinkles,
soothe me into believing I'm a writer.

Eight Reasons to Take a Walk on Sunday Morning ~ Margaret Simon

8. Bells chime a call to worship
to empty pews echoing the song of trees.

7. I'm sorry I keep taking the same path,
the same images do not grow weary of me noticing.

I pick gardenias from CeCe's side yard.
If she came out, she wouldn't mind.

6. I stop at Anne's to view her century plant as it reaches
skyward. A century plant waits 25 years to bloom,
blooming only once in a lifetime. A lifetime
I took for granted only weeks ago.

5. I can take my time.
No one will call to check on me.

I'll check the feeders:
the hummingbirds like sweet water.

I'll get to it in time.

4. I walk and walk
wondering if it will always be this way.

Hollow bells pealing for no one.

No one venturing out to see anyone.

3. It may rain tomorrow. Today,
the sun shines, the birds sing,
and I don't have to join the chorus.

I'll keep singing to myself.

2. A link was sent by email
to a video church service, one priest, one reader.

The organist plays
as though the cathedral is full.

Full feels scary now.
Full carries weight.
Who wants to be full?

1. I close this book,
heat another cup of tea,
and find my shoes,
find my way,
fill my day.
and perhaps...

Bloom!

A View From Forever Saturday ~
Margaret Simon

A change will be arriving here.
Come near.
The captive shell is broken free.
Follow me.
Someone will likely lose their way.
You may.
We're on the crest of a new day.
Fear should never capture your hand.
When Moon rises above this land.
Come near. Follow me. You may.

The Duplex of Virtual Teaching ~
Margaret Simon

Butterfly wings remind her of her mother
A monarch is held by a child's fingers

> A child's fingers hold her face before a screen
> The screen fades as she covers her mouth to speak

If she can fade by covering her mouth
no one will notice she is there

> No one will notice she is there
> or not there; activate the mute button

Activate mute speaks louder than words
In a virtual world, you may miss something

> In a virtual world, you may miss
> her hand reaching out to touch you

Her hand may reach out to touch you
like a mother's touch in butterfly wings

Magic Bean ~
Margaret Simon

How a writer is made
some think comes from a magic bean–
it just is
this writer can't help but write & write,
but I know better.
I know a writer comes from the magic wand
of a teacher who told her
she was.
A teacher finds magic
in the light of a child's words,
rubs the lantern again & again.
She knows the power of waiting,
of how a seed of an idea
can sprout
if you give it
nourishment
& time.

I love most
the smile of realization
"Wow! I wrote that!"
Pride from my wishing
which, in the end,
is me working magic,
still unknown,
still a mystery.

Shelter-In-Place ~
Donnetta Norris

Home Inside
Staying safe
Sanity wanes
Online learning links
Zoom video meetings
Writing to help clear my mind
Stretching myself with poetry
Uncertain of what will come of it
Hoping others will shelter-in-place too

Dear Online Learning, ~
Donnetta Norris

I realize that you are not a novelty, by any means.
You were the method by which I obtained my teaching degree.
But, it is so different having to be on the creative side,
rather than the user side.
I now have become the producer of online instruction, and
to be perfectly honest, this is hard.
I can only imagine how the parents of my Scholars must feel;
having to learn to navigate apps, usernames, passwords, and downloads.
Online Learning, are you here to stay?
Will this continue as the new landscape of education?
I hope not...I miss the smiles of my Scholars...
their hugs, high-fives, and hand shakes.
I know this is not your fault, Online Learning.
You are the result of something so sinister
that no one could have ever fathomed would occur
in our lifetime.
I guess, though, Online Learning, when I look on the bright side,
Many of us are learning new skills.

Incorporating "We Real Cool" by Gwendolyn Brooks ~ Donnetta Norris

We are doing hard things that are
Real hared to understand and have us losing our
Cool. Enhancing our skills sets so
We can deliver what our Scholars need. Having nothing
Left sometimes, but try as we might to keep
School as normal as possible.
We push online learning despite the fears that
Lurk beneath the surface of it all. Fearing it's too
Late to meet all their diverse needs.
We try to extend grace to ourselves and others as we
Strike against the status quo
Straight toward the unknown.
We are the champions of doing more with less. So, we
Sing our own praises for our valiant efforts. There is no
Sin in being unsure and pressing on when
We are ALL learning on the fly, because there's a
Thin line between…No! It's wide as hell. Trying to score like in
Gin Rummy and not lose this game.
We dig deep and search long and hard to
Jazz up our current circumstance. Praying we make it to
June. Uncertain of how long
We will work under these conditions…do or
Die, right or wrong. Longing for an end to this

Wake up – trod downstairs to make the drink that will give me energy ~
Donnetta Norris

Read and post the Scripture of the day – the Word of God gives me life
Practice Spanish via an app – hopefully I'll be fluent before I die
Read the corresponding date of my Daily Bible – there's no such thing as too much God
Pray
Workout for an hour or take a 3-mile walk – moving by body is important to me
Shower and dress – pajamas count, right?
Prepare breakfast and multitask for work – technically on the clock at 8:45
Review Scholarly work – plan for sending out more
Make contact with parents – try to make this hard thing simple…"do the best you can"
Emails, Emails – check and respond
Eat something that is supposed to be lunch – don't judge me
Continue the work cycle until I can't take it anymore – planning, reaching out to parents, reviewing activities, checking emails
As dusk approaches, but often not until the dark of night
I finally sit down away from the Must-do
Preparing my mind to focus on the Get-to-do, the Want-to-do
Notebook open, pens by my side
Drawing a blank on what to write

Taking Back a Wish ~
Angelica Braaten

Sad
Silence
No more sound
No more people
No more rickshaw bells
No more vehicle horns
No more deafening dog howls
What you wish for sometimes comes true
I wished for the constant noise to stop
I didn't realize noise equals life

Letter from Future Self ~
Angelica Braaten

Dear Angie in 2003,

You will have a birthday.
Your golden birthday.
Cherish it, write about it.
You will forget it if you don't.

You will love school but you'll also be
a little rebellious
You should probably stay
a "little" rebellious,
Nothing more.
I know it might be hard for a girl
who always follows the rules.
This will be the one year you do not like your English teacher,
but there's always something to learn.
And you will read a play
that you will teach in ten years.
Maybe pay more attention.
So you can compare and contrast.
And if you don't want to memorise the feel of benches,
you should practice more.

You will get to be a fish
in your backyard pool.
Enjoy it because while you are fifteen,
your parents will tell you that you are moving
to a different state
for the second time in your life.
Your brother will be enraged,
for good reason – he's a junior.
You will not say anything.
Please say something.
You never have strong opinions
and maybe you should.

They will ask you how you feel.
You will cry in your room alone
trying to figure out how you feel.
Somewhere in the middle, always.
Maybe just say that.

At fifteen, you will move to Louisiana
Cross country.
The cat you've had for sixish years will disappear
right before you leave.
And this is when you will know the feeling of having
no closure.
Maybe this is when your obsession
with knowing the truth is formed.
Where did he go?

You will go to a new school
Experience culture shock.
You will be malleable clay
Wanting to fit into everyone's hands
Shape yourself with your own hands.
You will be exposed to things
Only seen in movies.
You will need to figure out the balance
between being careful and being open.
Write about it.
You will forget it if you don't.

At fifteen, your dad will give you the keys
to his truck on New Year's Eve
and let you drive somewhere with your friend
even though you've never driven anywhere by yourself,
even though you don't have a license?
You will put one foot on each pedal
and know you won't die.
You will enjoy this freedom
and you will take advantage of it later.
Do not take advantage of it.

At fifteen, you will not live with your brother
for the first time in your life.
Too soon.
You will be happy for him,
you will be heartbroken.
It'll be ok…you'll live together again someday.
Not long after, you will no longer live with your grandma.
Not long after, you will no longer live with your dad.
Maybe make sure that's what you want.
It will somewhat shape your future.
Write about it.
You will forget it if you don't.

At fifteen, you will exchange "i love you" with some guy.
You will think you feel something like love.
Be careful,
many things feel like love at this age,
at the end of fifteen.

Love,
Angie in 2020

Detail of Swamp Forest ~
Angelica Braaten

Roots and branches crawling from water to sky,
like hundreds of hands raised to heaven.

When does your existence end?
A silent, shadowed maze tucked away.

Baptism in a cha milk tea river,
Everything works together here.

Follow the leader into the water,
Follow the leader out of the water.

You are meant to be exactly where you are,
Connected in wonder. Don't close your eyes.

Reciprocity ~
Angelica Braaten

Student is to teacher as
Trust is to relationship as
Universe is to me as
Dreams were to King as
Energy is to machine as
Nature is to artist as even
Teacher is to student.

Song Lyrics ~
Jamie Langley

if my words did glow with the gold of sunshine
song lyrics
ripple in still water
when there is no pebble tossed
nor wind to blow

on any given day, in any given moment
words ripple through
a sound track to life
a link to the moment

how the hell can a person go to work in the morning
and come home in the evening and have nothing to say
twenty year old me could never have imagined
how do people let go?

go to the country, build you a home
plant a little garden, eat a lot of peaches
not far from
our urban garden edged by peach trees

come on home
come on home
no you don't want to
be alone
just come on home
left me weeping thinking of Rachel
alone in Mexico City
in this time of corona

so easy for the words to ripple through

At the Table ~
Jamie Langley

facing the screen waiting for them to arrive
a candle flickers anchoring me to this space
as they arrive hellos are exchanged
and should we wait another minute to start
weather check-in brought lots of partly cloudy
this is how we talk when we share a table
intentions spoken patience, sustainability
motivation, relaxed fluid, schedule or not
conscious thought visible in faces
in the grid across my screen

so begins the last day of week one in the remote classroom

two show up for office hours
a little English talk about their reading – lots of time
happy to talk to familiar people
easy conversation, hey Ms Langley

the last class is small
class begun with how have you been doing
conversation was easy
we've been doing it for months
Kate shared a book talk missed the day class was canceled
a little talk about two stories, energy lacking
now faces frozen in squares
words are easy
but something is missing

Weather ~
Jamie Langley

On a morning in March I visited my classroom
to gather items from my classroom.
Not imagining time to be long, I watered
and left my plants on the bookshelves by the windows.
I discovered that during a pandemic I can get along
with fewer decisions. What to expect is clearly not
the lens we are using. The structure of a calendar
opens in new ways allowing space for personalization.
More for me in my life than the anticipated role of
personalization in my newly forming classes. I became
a practicing writer, as I led my students through weekly
essays preparing for an AP exam. One writer leading
many writers. I moved through April losing a favorite musician,
Passover for two, and no clear vision of what might be next.
What to expect is clearly not the lens we are using.
Before long it was May with traditional end of year landmarks
but without the structure of the days, of the weeks. Eleventh graders
waking up and coming together before logging on to a 45 minute
exam from the comfort of more than 80 bedrooms around the
city outscoring the students of the past in rows of tables and chairs
in a gymnasium. What to expect is clearly not the lens we are using.
Summer melted into a Dali-esque landscape until I accepted control
adding a workout to my days of walking dogs and writing.
School schedules as varied as the elastic ties I use to tie back my hair
came and went. I planned in fits and starts fed by antiracist ideas
for revisioning curriculum narrowing a focus. Online instruction
seasoned my thinking. Books took turns on my nightstand
filling my head and days. Tomorrow our faculty meets for the first day
to plan and learn about an upcoming year. What to expect
is clearly not the lens we are using.

Credo ~
Jamie Langley

a shift in my life left an empty space
I missed caring for her
a layer in my life lost

more natural with my daughters
the connection extends beyond words and space
though the umbilical cord has been cut

what they need is found intuitively
not through a great laid plan
is intuition led by the heart in the context of the head?

a lesson taught goes well
a hike to a desired summit
with an aging body, the desire to reach the destination keeps me going

the hoja santa leaves show me they survived the not so cold winter
mint sprawls out from its corner
they thrive as they push out from the soil

Salt Water Taffy ~
Jamie Langley

Mom stood at the stove
stirring the melting sugar
and watched the thermometer
the pot handle held by the mit

the light blond liquid
thickening by the spoon
a swirl of lines
led by the spoon
pulls the edges
from the sides of the pot

lightly buttered fingers
hold on to globs of hardened
sugar
pulling and pulling til
the strands grow thinner and lighter

strands of candy rest
on sheets of wax paper
waiting to harden
fine strands of candy
pulled between fingers
create a web of sugar touching every kitchen surface

Turn From Poem* ~
Denise Hill

I think I could turn
into the most kind
thoughtful loving
human being
filled with grace
and humility.

But each day
some new stupidity
has me kvetching
at the television
railing against the radio
muttering into my thoughts.

About the idiots
the selfish the negligent
the self-righteous
the willfully ignorant
and all their
kindred relations.

I studied meditation
and learned of meta
how to make phrases
to silence my worst critic
to accept others
just as they are.

Even to embrace
and show them
loving thoughts
like the Dalai Lama
who was exiled from
his own country.

Still he shows
compassion towards those
who demonize him
murder his people.
He only wants peace
and a safe return.

I am not the Dalai Lama.
I never believe I could turn
into anything nearly like him.
So each day I breathe
I seethe I reset I try again.
This is who I am.

*Inspired by Walt Whitman's "Song of Myself" Stanza 32 from Leaves of Grass, which begins,
"I think I could turn and live with animals, they are so placid and self-contain'd…"

Our Camelot ~
Denise Hill

That empty school and parking lot
normal when the season is hot
has weeds now grown in every crack
no students will be coming back
no building opened as it ought.

I sit instead in this one spot
behind the screen, it's all I've got
replacing solid mortared brick
that empty school.

My students' lives already fraught
resiliencies are all pulled taut
my promise I will not take back
to forge ahead, no afterthought
mythologize our Camelot
that empty school.

Indelible Moments ~
Denise Hill

It was the first day of school
after they found N.
on a wellness check at his home
he died sitting in his chair
cuppa tea left steeping in the kitchen
I had to meet his students
tell them he would not
be coming back
I asked them to take out
a blank sheet of paper
write down their thoughts and feelings
share if they wanted

It was the first day of school
after 9/11
I grappled to make sense
how to make any of it matter
whether anyone would
even show up
the class was full and silent
we opened our blank books
filled them with thoughts and feelings
we would all look back on
each decade later

It was the first day of school
after the pandemic
it hasn't yet arrived
but I can already understand
everything we've lost
everything I loved most
now the mounting fear
and resolve to make it work
each day I open my journal
make note of cases and deaths
locally and globally
so many thoughts and feelings
still yet to come

Elms on Death Row ~
Denise Hill

Three trees stand solemnly
in a row just as planted
nearly one hundred years ago

Each tendril root
tapped deeply into place
somnolently holding to earth

Craggy rough bark
like aged hands so many
life stories harbored there

Each now marked: a bright red dot
some roughshod city worker
sprayed just doing his job

Their days are numbered
soon hewn to stumps
then those ground flush

I place my hand on one
breathe in breath out
say "Thank you"

then the next: Thank you.
then the next: Thank you.

Lest they go from this world
unappreciated for all
they have provided.

Thank you.

Grounded ~
Ashley Valencia-Pate

My toes sink in red clay
bare feet against Earth
face upturned and
Heaven's light shining
I let the current run
mind, body, soul, back
into the gentle Earth–
Four elements intertwining.
Don't forget me please.
The balance must stay
We both have to connect
We both need each other
I ground myself and
promise to do my part,
to appreciate the beauty,
to mourn the loss of land.
Surrounded by an open field,
hawks looking at rabbits, cardinals
looking for worms, and I

looking up–grounded.

Feet to Night ~
Ashley Valencia-Pate

Pitter patter of paws
Pitter patter of feet
Feet bringing songs
Feet bringing dances
Dances that move us
Dances shaking the day
Day shines on a farm
Day embraces the fields
Fields filled with hunts
Fields filled with joy
Joy in kinder treasure
Joy in bird watching
Watching cardinals swoop
Watching dogs run
Run after rabbits
Run after wind
Wind spreading corn
Wind tempting deer

Deer musk and earth
Deer hiding watching
Watching the corn drop
Watching for red brass
Brass bound respectfully
Brass used humbly
Humbly from afar
Humbly with respect
Respect the animal
Respect the land
Land bigger than us
Land wiser and older
Older and gentle
Older and ornery

Ornery with stickers
Ornery with red clay
Red clay squishing
Red clay blowing dust

Dust speckling walls
Dust covering boys
Boys who run
Boys who imagine
Imagine a pirate ship
Imagine stadium lights
Lights of the future
Lights from magic bugs
Bugs that mesmerize
Bugs who signal night
Night falls quietly
Night brings them in
In to the table
Quietly like thunder

Give Me A Beat ~
Ashley Valencia-Pate

Give me a beat
    Sharp notes to wake
Give me a beat
Crescendos to create
Give me a beat
A pause not too long
Give me a beat
A moment for a song
I just need to make a sound
To rise up, out, to resonate
I just need to get a little loud
To push open this gate
I just need this anger found
To hit the coda and melt away

    Give me a room
Acoustics with arms open
Give me a room
A voice like an explosion
Give me a room
I know I'm not broken
I just need to make a sound
To rise up, out, to resonate
I just need to get a little loud
To push open this gate
I just need this anger found
To hit the coda and melt away

Keep This Fire Burning Steady ~
Ashley Valencia-Pate

Sweet girl, I am standing ready
Let me examine your tribute
Keep this fire burning steady
Mmm, I can smell those veggies
I sense the stickiness of the fruit
Sweet girl, I am standing ready
I think those onions are getting sweaty
Stop worrying, googling for a substitute
Keep this fire burning steady
I must say, you are quite messy
Sloshing sticky sauces, I need a wetsuit
Sweet girl, I am standing ready.
I have a flame, a power I levy
The propane climbing up my root
Keep this fire burning steady.
See how those flavors marry?
What can my magic execute?
Sweet girl, I am standing ready.
Keep this fire burning steady.

Thoughts While Waiting for the Board of Education's Decision of What Will Happen in the Fall
Or
The 5 Es Lesson Plan in the Time of COVID-19 ~
Scott McCloskey

Etymology --
Does school need to be
face-to-face? Does direct
instruction mean we are actually
in the same room, together?
Does school mean "the building,"
the brick and mortar -- built
in the 1950s, faulty HVac system --
building? The word school comes
from the Greek meaning leisure
and philosophy and, yes, it also
means lecture place, but the
Google definition mentioned
leisure first, so we'll highlight
that and besides "where I
lecture" isn't as important as
where the "learning" takes place:
In the minds of my students. So,
in your face Aristotle -- and don't
get me started on the absurd notion
(and hugely problematic practice)
of requiring all kids to wear uniforms,
to sit up straight at their desks -- in their
home offices? -- while leaving their
Zoom cameras on.

Entomology --
Which leads me to the question,
what do these people -- the over
200 people in this Zoom,
their little faces -- or, as in this case
over 80% have their own cameras off --
just white names on black backgrounds --

what do these people think happens
In a school? Do they think we are all
Just worker ants, marching along,
lock step, all curricular activities
the same, being met and performed the
same way. Or to put it another way,
do they have this collective hive mind
thinking schools are safe because
they read it in their Facebook feed?

Ecology --
Have they never met a teenager
or a group of them working in
concert? Do they not remember
the PDAs In the hallways, the sitting
together outside classrooms, the
packed stairwells. Students
clump. They cluster. They take
back their agency when they can
to oppose the dreaded seating charts
and forced group work so often
imposed upon them.

Epidemiology --
And yet everyone now is an
expert on this disease, on
The effectiveness of masks
or face coverings, and yet,
still, we see so many people
wearing them incorrectly,
noses out, just hanging in the
wind, -- or, perish the thought --
not wearing one at all, believing
it is their constitutional right
to spread their (possible) infections
to anyone and everyone to whom
they see fit.

So, yeah, we come to Epistemology.
That's right. I said it -- hard emphasis
on the second syllable -- because
I'm angry now -- waiting on pins
and needles -- our very own bug
board -- for these seven people
to do what's right, what makes the
most sense and is safest for everyone
involved. So, I wait, listening
for the roll call that will determine
my fate,
which, of course,
is from Latin
meaning 'that which
has been spoken.'

Prose Poem with a Horse ~
Scott McCloskey

You can lead a high school senior to poetry but you can't make him drink. I
want to sidestep (or sidepass, as the case may be) the problematic imagery
of student as horse, but I can't, because it's at the root of the issue -- there
I go switching again -- so it goes (shout out to Vonnegut Jr.), so yesterday,
really, yesterday, as in the day before today, this aforementioned horse student
(centaur?) says he didn't like the poem we read, didn't think "words of
encouragement" were enough in the world, if you wanted to help someone
you should give them a hand or, even better, give them money, not write some
dumb poem. Wait, so, does this poor creature really think that Nikki Giovanni
is talking about spiders? Or e.e. cummings and a mouse? Or Maxine Kumin
and woodchucks? Or, perish the thought, but that Elizabeth Bishop just
really liked to fish? Stafford's poem is NOT about a (pregnant) dead doe on
the side of the road. I mean, yes, of course it is, of course they are, but they
are all about so much more. So much more. We're talking about "imaginary
gardens" with "real toads" in them here! And hat tip to WCW because we
overlook that to our peril, and, I think, it was this, that my student didn't
understand, he is just scratching the surface, pawing his hoof on the ground to
mimic the arithmetic of logic, but not digging deeper, not plumbing his inner
depths, which is, ultimately, perhaps, what great poetry can do for us (to hold
a "mirror up to nature" and show us the inmost part of ourselves), and I realize
that amidst all the craziness and horror of this current moment -- this is my
job, this is what I signed on for, so I roll up my sleeves, mop my brow -- what?
thinking about the work is sometimes more exhausting than the work itself --
grab for Seamus Heaney's spade and start to dig.

Slaughter-House Five by Kurt Vonnegut Jr.
"Allowables" by Nikki Giovanni
"Me Up at Does" by e.e. cummings
"Woodchucks" by Maxine Kumin
"The Fish" by Elizabeth Bishop
"Traveling through the Dark" by William Stafford
"Poetry" by Marianne Moore
"Asphodel, That Greeny Flower" by William Carlos Williams
Hamlet by Shakespeare
"Digging" by Seamus Heaney

Note from Scott about the poem: And the poem he didn't "like"? "The Miracle of Morning" by
Amanda Gorman

(re)Looking ~
Scott McCloskey

I have a confession.

I don't really like Wallace Stevens.
I know, right? I'm a monster.

I can appreciate his place
in capital "L" literature; I just don't
know if I understand it -- his poetry,
not his place (but, I guess, I don't under
stand that either).

I've tried, believe me,
I've taken classes on modern poetry,
I've read half a biography on the dude,
listened to lectures and podcasts
raving about his "Anecdote of the
Jar" (which seems like he just didn't
pick up after himself. It seems, to all
accounts, that Wallace is just a litter
bug. He left a jar in Tennessee
and wrote a poem about it. Cool.) or
his "The Emperor of Ice-Cream" (which, yes,
I guess is about a prostitute or something,
sure, but it has nothing to do with Rocky Road
or Ben and Jerry's Chunky Monkey) and
this leads me to his blackbird poem,
the one about "looking."

(I'd much rather, to be honest, spend my time
listening to "Blackbird" by The Beatles --
which I currently am, by the way, -- and
"Blackbird fly into the light of a dark black
night" is so much better than "I was of three
minds, / Like a tree / In which there are
three blackbirds." What?! LOL. Seems
like lazy writing, Wallace.)

(I mean, I know, I know,
he's Mr. Wallace Stevens,
preeminent American poet, heralded in countless
hallowed halls, winner of the Pulitzer Prize
in 1955, and, I, on the other hand,
once had a poem in the local college's lit mag, so
we're on equal footing, is what I'm trying to say.)

And my thoughts are as valued (and valuable?)
as his, if reader-response literary criticism is
to be believed, but this is not what I'm
thinking about at the moment.

What I'm thinking about at the moment
is why am I in an office hour Zoom call
all by myself.

I've got the Zoom window open, and I'm
looking at myself, *looking* at myself, contemplating
the choices that I made to get here.

Don't get excited,
they're nothing heady
nor profound.

I was just wondering about "looking." And about
Wallace Stevens. When I felt a tickle in
my nose -- my left nostril to be exact -- so I
tilted my head backward and flared those
suckers for all they're worth

when I realized
that I didn't hit pause
on the recording.

So now, there's film of me checking
my nose on camera and I wonder, not
for the first time mind you,
if Edgar Allan Poe had to worry about nose
hairs or Paul McCartney, or, heaven forbid,
even Mr. Wallace Stevens himself.

They all have noses, right? And presumably
they all have hairs in their, respective, noses.

So did, say, Sylvia Plath, ever, mid thought, mid
sentence even, hold her pen aloft (line of verse
momentarily forgotten) crane her head backward,
eyes gently closed as if to ward off a sneeze,
only to vigorously rub her nose trying to dislodge
a foriegn body?

Had Emily Dickinson ever wondered aloud,
"Because I could not stop for Death --
He kindly stopped for WHAT IS IN MY NOSE?!"

I can almost picture Wallace digging his
meaty fingers into each nostril -- forefinger
and thumb vying for purchase -- to forcefully
tug on his nasal septum, all the while, thinking,
Can I write a poem about a wayward nose
hair?

These are the things I think about when I'm
sitting in a Zoom 'room" by myself, staring at
myself, *staring* at myself

until, of course, I realize I am an hour early
for the meeting.

Washing Hands ~
Scott McCloskey

They say that all poems are
political; all poems are
an expression of freedom
against oppression are
innately radical. Their
mere "existence is
resistance."

But not this one.

This one is just about me
washing my hands
and how sometimes I lose
count, so I need to start
over to ensure that
I've done it for the proper
length of time.

Hands lathered up, I stare
out the kitchen window
at the neighbor's house,
at my neighbor who, although
it's the middle of December,
and sure, it is unseasonably
warm, looks to be planting fake
flowers in the sills outside
of her windows.

This is the same neighbor
who was surprised when her
racist lawn ornaments were
stolen this past summer
when yet more videos
of atrocities and injustices
were going viral,

which, of course, makes me
scrub more vigorously, thinking
of the UPS package that came,
the actual reason that I'm standing
here in the kitchen --
Was that one thousand seventeen
or eighteen? --

So, I apply more soap from the
hands free dispenser, and
watch, transfixed, as she carefully,
artistically even, places various
colors and kinds together, creating,
to her mind at least, a pleasing
arrangement, taking more care
and effort to arrange these fake
flowers than she has ever
afforded her neighbors.

And I just wanted to wash my
hands, wanted to not (potentially)
infect my wife or myself, wanted
to simply go about my business,
maybe read a little, grade an essay
or two,

but I keep thinking
about the sad fact that
cultivation does take
time and effort and
persistence, and,
for some, it really
is easier to arrange
plastic flowers

than to plant
and nurture
live ones.

A Spring Credo ~
Alex Berkley

Happiness is easy
Like the still weeds we saw
Standing in a pond that looked like
Green Jell-O
The geese with their feet in the air
Fishing under a sun that seemed to be
Hurtling towards the surface

If I hear nothing but your laughter
And our puppy's snores
For the rest of my life
I'll miss music, for sure
But I guess I'd be okay

We walked back on a muddy path
With our baby son on your back
Deer watching with placid fear

The humans here are okay, they say
Except maybe that guy on the bench
Who has the mild look of a serial killer
But perhaps we're stereotyping
And he's probably a fine guy
Just enjoying the sunshine

Then ~
Alex Berkley

Then,
We walked
Finally
Back to real life
Weeks told in headlines:
"People Free To Do Things"
"Life To Be White Noise Again"
Papers sell like hotcakes today
But I notice eyes searching the sky
Waiting for metaphorical asteroids

Blue ~
Alex Berkley

You have blue eyes
clearly from your mother
since my eyes are brown.

And I always thought
everyone in my family
had brown eyes

until you were born
and my mom pointed out
my dad's eyes are bright blue too.

Sometimes in the mornings
you look at me from your crib
with narrowed eyes and a furrowed brow.

You look so grumpy to be waking up
but it's like,
kid,
it's not even 6am

and your mama and I have
no problem with you staying
asleep for another hour.

But those blue eyes are piercing.

They remind me of my dad
in old black and white photos
from the '60s
when he was relatively new too.

When your eyes laugh
it is your mama's laughter
echoing across a canyon of time.

I don't see me yet
but I don't need to.

You are everyone I love.

Day One ~
Alex Berkley

We sat in
The yard on
A blanket while
Clem crawled around
Exploring
A uniquely warm March
Afternoon

The winters
Can be so
Long

But when
The Sun starts
To shine

Everyone starts to
Barbecue and play
Music on old boomboxes
In their yards

And everyone starts to
Drink with
A celebratory tone

In stark contrast to
Our February drinking
Which is done purely
To beat back
The misery
Of brown snow on
The roadside and
God's gray
Middle finger
Up in the sky

I watched Clem's face
As he studied
A twig in his fingers

And I thought about
Thursday
When I
Stopped at a red light
And received a
Washington Post update
On my phone:
Ohio was closing
All
Of their schools

It took
Until Monday morning
For New York to
Shut
Down

Karen walked into the backyard
With a bag of popcorn
And two bowls

"In true social distancing fashion"
She said
Handing one bowl
To Kayleigh

We all sipped
Wine and looked up at a blue
Sky when I felt my phone
Buzz again:

"California issues stay at
Home order in the
Bay area"

I felt calm.

I texted Sean
In San Francisco

I watched Clem
Crawling faster towards
The gate

I felt Spring in
My lungs
And I tried to understand
That this
Was only the
Beginning

But to see
A beginning
In relation to some
Unknown end
Through a chasm of time
That doesn't even exist yet

Well,
Where do you even
Begin?

I took
A handful of popcorn
And finished
My wine

This was only
Day One

Pushing a Stroller ~
Alex Berkley

In the aftermath of a rainy day
Paints a little portrait of the zeitgeist

The runners who
Curve onto the road
Keeping six feet distance

The angry bald man
With a mask hanging round his neck
(And black knee socks reaching to his shorts)
Yelling at a barking dog through somebody's window

The park so beautiful and green
Dotted yellow with dandelions
Kids rapping while riding bikes
Making weird eye contact through windshields
Expressions masked

And we walk the loop round the perimeter
And there's an old man smoking and eating a sandwich
There are people walking dogs
Couples holding hands

Before you know it, there's actually some blue in the sky
Like Bob Ross just changed his mind about something
I watch Clem stretching in the stroller

It's actually getting hot
I take off his hat

And push the stroller home

Hello Pandemic ~
Jennifer Sykes

Covid-19
Global Pandemic
Fear of the unknown
Haunts our minds
Yet some seem unscathed
Think it's all a hoax
Is this real? Will it "all go away"?
I will be prepared.
I'll go with my gut.
THIS JUST IN: National State of Emergency
Thank God I followed my gut
Never trust the ignorant.
Everything's different, yet
The mind persists,
Still fearing.
The Anxieties of February well within reach,
While Nightmares of March introduce themselves
To the Succubus of April,
occupying the empty desk
At the front of my virtual classroom
I snicker at the vision,
But I'm not even sleeping.

Ending among Comfort ~
Jennifer Sykes

Trust in the Lord
Trust that an ending
Ending is a beginning
Beginning new ways of teaching
Teaching unfamiliar ways of learning
Learning meaningful lessons
Lessons of staying still
Still is the only way to move
Move forward during this time
Time seems to be crawling
Crawling further
Further into the unknown
Unknown to humankind
Humankind finds solitude
Solitude in the stillness
Stillness in quarantine
Quarantine allows new experiences
Experiences between parents and their children
Children and their school teachers
Teachers become students
Students overnight
Overnight developing lessons
Lessons from a distance
Distance unsought
Unsought and unbearable
Unbearable to see your friends
Friends and teachers on a screen
Screen creates a barrier
A barrier that protects
Protects yet causes grief
Grief of separation
Separation from those you love
Love transforms
Transforms into enrichment
Enrichment in art, music, reading, and writing
Writing crayoned messages and friendly letters

Letters with paintings and stories
Stories read on front porches
Porches that clasp those deliveries
Deliveries of outstretched arms
Arms that carry invisible hugs
Hugs that provide strength
Strength for the journey
Journey into the unknown
Unknown we must accept
Accept and seek comfort
Comfort and grace
Grace that is necessary
Necessary
Grace

World Awakens ~
Jennifer Sykes

The world awakens
buds of yellow, green, and pink
Start to peak out from their hiding places
Beads of rain rest on the reclining sticks,
Victims of the sleds that pummeled over them
While resting.
Daily walks to the mailbox
Bring recycling bin food,
And the whisper of poppy hellos and lily bulb salutations
Bring a much needed smile to my face.
A chill catches me off guard
While the sun's rays stroke my spine
Warmth.
Finds its home and
Decides to stay a bit longer each night.
Raindrops dot the ground
stirring up the dust
The smell of wet soil, and rotting worms
That couldn't find their way back
Escort me on my return
Preparing the way for summer lust.
It will be here soon.
It must!

After Viewing "Young boys harassing the first African American family to move into the all-white neighborhood" ~
Glenda Funk

Last night I dreamed I saw a
young Don harassing the first
African American family
moving into his all-white
neighborhood. He stretched
tiny fists in raised rage,
spittle foaming from his mouth—
a circle wrapped around his hate—
bellowing a bubbling brew,
feeding a klan of kreepy kids,
misfits like him from a
Flannery O'Connor short story
who believe in jesus and justice,
just not the god of love. His
barbed-wire words stretch
like a cabled line reaching across
history into infinity,
still measuring others
not by *the content of their*
character but by the color of
their skin, their *shit-hole* homes.
Now a squinting shadow
stands spewing and shoveling
the same slop, while
around the resolute desk
the boys swarm.
He ain't learned nothing.
And so it goes.
Who knew in this
child a good man
would be so
hard to find?

Note from Glenda about the poem:*Additional inspiration from Eve Ewing's "I saw Emmitt Till this week at the grocery store," and Lorraine Hansbury's "A Raisin in the Sun."

Simultaneous Concurrent Action ~
Glenda Funk

Bodies
belonging to no one:
Unclaimed
Anonymous
Alien lifeless forms
Abandoned,
Left like
Refuse stacked
Awaiting burial in
Mass graves on
Hart Island---
Interred by
Hazmat suit-clad diggers.
Meanwhile...
Covid-19 infected
Nurses---
First Responders---
Tend the infirm,
Themselves gravely
Ill---infected---
Unable to procure
PPE through
Flatlined supply chains
Unlinked==broken==disconnected;
Vital skills more
Requisite than
Vital signs.

Poetry Shifts ~
Glenda Funk

First the morning crew arrives
Eager wordsmiths,
Morning birds
Pecking about the nest,
Excited for the daily
Worm, prompts dangling before
Hungry ravenous beaks;
Fluttering hummingbirds
Sucking nectar-engorged lines
They flit and fly in and
Out of the nest as
Sundials twirl, words swirl.

Dusk yawns and
Stretches its tired rays
Across a pink horizon
Signaling an awakening;
Night owls emerge in
Silent flight & nestle in the nest.
They hoot and perch on
High canto branches;
Their hawkish eyes revolve,
Clocking, Observing,
Expelling feathery runes of
Poesy upon a word-wonder world.

Skin ~
Lauryl Bennington

Smooth, perfect, porcelain skin
But it wasn't mine.
Mine was freckled with red dots
Varying in size and space.
I stared at the large picture on Vogue's cover;
I glared in the overwhelming mirror in my bathroom.
I compared the two images.
Even though there isn't a book on what beauty is or means,
I always knew that wasn't me.
My mom tells me not to worry,
"You'll grow out of it," she says.
But what usually only happens to teens
Still happens to me as an adult.
My family all share olive tones and even textures.
My skin is scarred and cracking under the pressure,
but somehow increasingly oily at the same time.
Medicine bottles and ointments crowd my bathroom counter.
Still full from weeks without use.
They never work anyways.
Tears fall rapidly into my large oval pores.
If only those were a magical serum;
My skin would be flawless and glowing.

Introvert ~
Lauryl Bennington

Introverted personality,
I always longed for my alone time.
Every time I was stuck in a crowd
Stiff, uncomfortable, just wanting to go home
Curl up with a book
And my own simple thoughts.
Now my thoughts are too much alone
I find myself reaching for the phone
Begging for connection that I loathed before
The touch of a hand,
The brush of a shoulder,
Even a hug.
Why oh why did you always want to be alone
Was it because you had a choice to be with people
Was it because you actually wanted to be alone
Now it seems
My longing has changed from one to many

Coffee ~
Lauryl Bennington

Having a morning coffee with you
is something we've never done,
But I can picture it perfectly.
Laughter would echo as you poured,
Steam would rise from the mug,
Yours would be black and mine a light brown.
We'd be sitting criss-cross on the couch,
Windows open letting in the breeze,
Sipping lightly as the caffeine awakens us.
Maybe someday we can share a morning coffee.
Until then, I'll enjoy this cup of joe on my own thinking of you.

Dear Lauryl, ~
Lauryl Bennington

At fifteen you wanted to be an actress on Broadway, or even better at the West End. Even before then, you wanted to be a journalist but always had a knack for too much detail that journalism would never allow. While some paths have now taken you down different directions you wouldn't change where your life is now and where you are headed. You should've always known you were going to become a teacher after you played school every day as a child and you were never the designated student.

At fifteen you blasted Taylor Swift love songs in the passenger seat of your mom's green Ford Broncho as if you had been heartbroken by a million different boys. Nothing felt more cathartic than blasting "White Horse" down I-35 with the windows slightly cracked and hair flying in a multitude of different directions. Your music taste has definitely changed now, but you still crave that highway drive. It's only you and the road now though.

At fifteen you were hurt by too many mean girls in school, but just hold on a little longer until you are able to reach your life-long best friends in college. Everything you went through before will be worth the torture just to even meet these wonderful people. You will feel like you've known them your whole life and college will fly by in the blink of an eye.

At fifteen you could've never envisioned how your life is now. How different things are from your imagination. I think if there is one lesson you should carry with you is to expect the unexpected and to embrace change. Change is the only constant now. I know you are a control freak and love to be in charge of everything, but sometimes it's okay to just go with the flow. Embrace everything in life: the good, the bad, and the wildly fanciful and unexpected.

Best wishes,

Lauryl

Time Limerick ~
Lauryl Bennington

There is a man who is named time.
He is quite fond of doing crime.
Thievery more so;
Prying in to cause woe.
Hear him now. His incessant chime.

Teacher-Poets

Abigail M. Woods is 21 years old and currently attends Oklahoma State University; she is anticipating graduation in December of 2021. She is studying Secondary English Education and minoring in English (Creative Writing). She has been working in education for four years with all age groups. Abigail spends her summers working at Camp Waldo in West Virginia. She spends her free time hiking with her dog McGee, hammocking with a good book, and fishing from her kayak. Abigail has previously been published in *Dissonance Magazine* and will have work appearing in the *Red Dirt 2021 Anthology*.

Alex Berkley is a high school special education teacher from Buffalo, New York. He has been teaching for 7 years. Alex is also a singer/songwriter with several self-released albums available on his bandcamp page. He likes to implement music in his curriculum because of its success with his students' performance. He enjoys spending time with his wife and son.

Allison Berryhill teaches English and journalism in Atlantic, Iowa. She is a publications-coordinator for the Iowa Council of Teachers of English. Her sonnets have been awarded first place in the Iowa Poetry Association's Lyrical Iowa competition in 2019 and 2020. Her 2020 sonnet was nominated for a Pushcart Prize. Follow her on Twitter @allisonberryhil for photos of #IowaSky and schoolblazing.blogspot.com for essays, where she has been chronicling over 300 days of the COVID-19 pandemic.

Andy Schoenborn is an award-winning author and high school English teacher in Michigan at Mt. Pleasant Public Schools. He focuses his work on progressive literacy methods including student-centered critical thinking, digital collaboration, and professional development. He is a past-president of the Michigan Council of Teachers of English, teacher consultant for the Chippewa River Writing Project, and Region Rep for the Michigan Reading Association. His first book, co-authored with Dr. Troy Hicks, *Creating Confident Writers*, was published in 2020. Follow him on Twitter @aschoenborn.

Angelica Braaten is from Dallas, Texas and taught high school English in Louisiana for 5 years. She decided she wanted to teach internationally and ended up moving to Dhaka, Bangladesh. Ms. Braaten is currently teaching middle school English at International School Dhaka. She has incorporated more poetry in her classroom and has had a great response from her students.

Anna J. Small Roseboro, a National Board Certified Teacher has over four decades of experience in public, private schools and colleges, mentoring early career educators, facilitating leadership institutes, in five states. She has served as director of summer programs and chair of her English department, published six textbooks based on these experiences, and was awarded Distinguished Service Awards by the California Association of Teachers of English and the National Council of Teachers of English. Her poetry appears in several issues of *Fine Lines: An Anthology of Poetry and Prose* (2015-2020) and has published *Experience Poems and Pictures: Poetry that Paints/Pictures that Speak* (2019).

Ashley Valencia-Pate currently resides in Perkins, Oklahoma. Over the past four years, Ashley has taught English at Stillwater High School. She felt a calling for teaching from a very early age through storytelling. She enjoys her school environment and being part of the community. She advocates for flexible curriculum and the growth that develops in students.

Barb Edler has taught English for the last forty years in Iowa, the last thirty in Keokuk where she encouraged students to find their own voice while taking risks, coaching speech participants, and supporting NHD competitors. Although retiring from teaching at Keokuk in 2020, she remains active instructing college composition courses. Barb enjoys watching the Mississippi roll by, reading, writing, playing cards, watching birds, and appreciating the simple things in life.

Betsy Jones lives and teaches in Moultrie, Georgia. In her ninth year as a full-time teacher, Betsy is currently an Academic Coach and 7th grade ELA Remote Learning teacher; she has taught Literature/Composition and Drama to 9th through 11th graders. Before accepting the call to become a teacher, she supervised tutoring programs in California; waited tables in South Georgia cafes; mentored students for high school graduation; taught English in Tegucigalpa, Honduras; and managed an independent bookstore. She is a life-long reader, writer, and self-professed "word nerd."

Denise Hill is a Michigander who ventured to Oregon for a few years before returning to the Mitten State. She has been in education in one way or another since kindergarten and hopes to close on thirty years as a college English teacher. Denise is also Editor of NewPages.com, an online resource for readers and writers, where she curates publication and contest guides for young writers.

Denise Krebs has been writing poetry with students for decades. However, last April was the first time she joined other teachers in a poetry-writing community, the first time she embraced the practice herself. Denise holds a master's degree in elementary education with a concentration in teaching reading. She teaches English to Arabic-speaking fifth graders in the first modern school in Bahrain, which started in 1899. Her one word for 2020 was TIME. Little did she know the Coronavirus would give her more time to just be. Besides enjoying the solitude and relaxing after too many years of so much doing, she also keeps busy reading, telling Bible stories, cooking and baking. @mrsdkrebs

Donnetta Norris resides in Mansfield, Texas and is a 2nd grade teacher with Arlington ISD. She has been an educator for the last 12 years. She is a graduate of Bowling Green State University (BSBA), Webster University (MAHRM), and Western Governors University (Post-Baccalaureate Teaching Certification). She is passionate about, and committed to, improving her writing craft as a teacher-writer as well as a writing teacher. She is a community leader and facilitates workshops with TeachWrite, LLC.

Emily Yamasaki lives in San Diego, California and has been teaching for 10 years in the public school system. She currently teaches sixth grade math and science. Emily studied Psychology and Education at the University of California, San Diego and continued to earn her Masters in Education from University of California, Los Angeles. Emily is a fellow and teacher consultant with the San Diego Area Writing Project with the National Writing Project.

Gayle Sands lives in Taneytown, Maryland, a small town just south of Gettysburg, PA. She retired from 27 rewarding years as an English teacher/Reading Specialist in local middle schools in July of 2020. She earned a 1978 BS in psychology (which allowed her to work in retail) and a career-change MA in Elementary Education. She has always loved words, and writing has been a source of pleasure and pride to her.

Glenda Cowen-Funk retired from a 38 year career as a classroom teacher of English and speech communication. Glenda is a National Board Certified Teacher in Young Adulthood English Language Arts. She holds a MA in English literature from Idaho State University. During her career Glenda coached forensics at Highland High School in Pocatello, Idaho, where she taught from 1989-2019. She taught two years in Iowa at Urbana Community School and began her career at Kofa High School in Yuma, Arizona, where she taught from 1981-1984 and 1986-1989. Her experience includes teaching AP Literature and Composition and working as an adjunct instructor for Idaho State U in the Early College Program. Glenda has been blogging since 2010 at https://evolvingenglishteacher.blogspot.com and has written for *California English*, but she only began writing poetry in March, 2018.

Jamie Langley teaches in Austin, Texas. She has taught in Austin for more than 25 years. Currently she teaches AP Language and Composition and 9th grade Pre-AP ELA. She teaches at the Ann Richards School for Young Women Leaders, a public girls school in Austin where she also serves as English department chair. Jamie is a graduate of Vanderbilt University and completed course work at the University of Texas in Austin to gain teacher certification. She has been a part of the New Jersey Writing Project in the past and currently a part of the National Writing Project through the University of Texas, Heart of Texas Writing Project.

Jennifer Guyor Jowett is an educator from Lansing, Michigan. Having attained her degree from Aquinas College in Grand Rapids, MI, she has taught for thirty years, mainly as a middle school ELA educator. She believes writing is a form of artistic expression and participating in a writing community allows teachers to speak authentically as writers with their students.

Jennifer Sykes, a 14-year veteran of the ELA classroom in Lansing, Michigan, has spent her years so far with 7th and 8th grade students at a large Catholic school. Her love for writing developed in middle school when she was introduced to strong female characters like Hermione Granger in the *Harry Potter* Series and started imitating poetry of strong female writers like Maya Angelou. Jennifer also finds great inspiration from music and lyrics that follow poetic forms. She believes that giving students the opportunity to write gives them the opportunity to share their voice.

Kate Currie is originally from suburban Chicago and currently resides in Florence, South Carolina. She serves English Department Chair and Associate Athletic Director and teaches juniors and seniors. Also, she serves as an academic advisor for the athletic programs. She holds a BA in Literary Studies and a MEd in Secondary English Education from DePaul University. She is currently working on her EdD in Curriculum and Instruction from University of South Carolina.

Katrina Morrison teaches 10th and 12th grade English in Skiatook, Oklahoma. This year marks her 15th year in the classroom. Katrina graduated from the University of Oklahoma with a BA in English and a minor in German. She earned a Master of Science in Higher Education Leadership from Northeastern University in Broken Arrow, Oklahoma. Katrina loves to read, write, read about writing, and write about reading.

Kimberly Johnson, EdD, is the District Literacy Specialist at Pike County Schools in Zebulon, Georgia. She has taught at all levels from Pre-K through high school. Kim enjoys participating in the monthly Open Writes at www.ethicalela.com and sees life's adventures through the lens of written expression.

Laura Langley lives in Little Rock, Arkansas. She graduated from Hendrix College in 2010 with a Bachelor's in Film Studies and received a Master's in Secondary Education from the University of Arkansas at Little Rock in 2017. She is currently in her sixth year of teaching high school English Language Arts, and this year she has juniors and seniors in a "blended learning environment." While she has fancied herself as a writer since middle school, she found her confidence as a writing teacher. One of her classroom goals is to help her students find their writing confidence and voices.

Lauryl Bennington is a Secondary Education: English major and pre-service teacher at Oklahoma State University and is from Edmond, Oklahoma. She plans to teach in a middle or high school upon graduation. She connects to writing through music, teaching others poetry, and by journaling constantly!

Linda Mitchell is a family girl, teacher-librarian in a public middle school and writes when she can get a word in edgewise. She received her BA from Ithaca College, MS from State University of New York at Geneseo, and a certificate from the University of Virginia --Wise. Creative writing is a joy that helps her figure out life.

Maureen Young Ingram lives and writes in Silver Spring, Maryland. She taught preschool for twenty years and mentored adults in their work with young children. Now retired, she is particularly proud of her years as founding faculty at a Washington, D.C. public charter. Maureen has a M.A. in International Studies, a B.A. in Political Science and Russian, and Early Childhood Certification. Maureen enjoys writing poetry about children, family, and nature.

Margaret Simon lives on the Bayou Teche in New Iberia, Louisiana. Margaret has been an elementary school teacher for 34 years and currently teaches ELA to gifted students. She has a masters in Education and National Board Certification. UL Press published her first book of children's poetry, *Bayou Song: Creative Explorations of the South Louisiana Landscape*. Margaret writes a blog regularly at http://reflectionsontheteche.com.

Melissa Ali is a coordinator at an elementary school in Los Angeles, California. She is the magnet coordinator, English language development coordinator, Title I coordinator, trauma-informed coordinator, and student empowerment coach. She also works as a consultant to help private schools de-colonize their curriculum. Melissa finds relief in her poetry.

Mo Daley has taught preschool through high school, ELA, Spanish, and reading. She is a middle school reading specialist in south suburban Chicago. Mo is a graduate of the University of Illinois and has been teaching for 27 years. She holds masters degrees in English and as a reading specialist. She loves writing and sharing her poetry.

Monica Schwafaty of Redondo Beach, California has been teaching for 26 years. She teaches 8th grade ELA. Monica has a Bachelor's Degree in English and Portuguese and a Masters Degree in Literary Education. Writing has always been an outlet for her; it's where she escapes to and processes her feelings and thoughts.

Sarah J. Donovan, Ph.D., is a former junior high language arts teacher of fifteen years and current assistant professor of secondary English education at Oklahoma State University. She is the author of *Genocide Literature in Middle and Secondary Classrooms* (2016) and the young adult novel in verse, *Alone Together* (2018).

Scott McCloskey, from Monroe, Michigan, has been teaching English Language Arts at the secondary level for 26 years and as a part-time adjunct at a community college for 20 years. When not in the classroom, he enjoys reading and writing and spending time with his wife. He writes (and reads) poetry because he has yet found no better way to understand himself or humanity than by reading and writing poetry.

Seana Hurd Wright is from Los Angeles, California. Seana has been teaching for 30 years primarily in the elementary sector. She is a National Board Certified Teacher and has taught all grades. She has been fascinated with writing since middle school and actually wrote a soap opera-ish novel with a friend in 7th grade that was silly yet exhilarating. Writing has always been natural and easy for her, and she's grateful to be able to share her thoughts in this anthology.

Shaun Ingalls lives in Las Vegas, Nevada and is entering his 25th year of teaching. Shaun currently teaches high school English. He received his BA in English with a minor in Middle East Studies from the University of Utah, completed his Secondary Education degree and Theatre education endorsement from Westminster College, and received his M.Ed. in Educational Leadership from University of Nevada Las Vegas. Writing during the pandemic has been a way for him to connect with others and better understand himself.

Stacey Joy, a native of Los Angeles, California, has been an elementary school teacher for 35 years. Stacey is a National Board Certified Teacher and currently teaches multiple subjects in 5th grade. She received her bachelor's degree from UCLA and her master's degree from CSUDH. Stacey has been writing poetry most of her life but being a fellow of the U.C.L.A. Writing Project helped her connect her writing with her teaching practice.

Stefani Boutelier, Ph.D., is an associate professor of education at Aquinas College in Grand Rapids, Michigan. Most of her K-12 classroom teaching was at the secondary level in Southern California, but she has worked at all levels of education for nearly 20 years. Her published works are in both academic and creative genres.

Susan Ahlbrand is in her 34th year of teaching 8th grade ELA in the small southern Indiana town of Jasper. A 1988 graduate of Indiana University, she has always written along with her students. That habit was heightened during the COVID 19 stay-at-home order when she fully participated in #verselove (an online poetry-writing community) as a way of processing the multitude of emotions being experienced.

Susie Morice, a retired educator in St. Louis, Missouri, has been working in various capacities in the field of education. She is a 30-year veteran of the public classroom and was a district leader in language literacy and gifted education. She has taught English Language Arts at the middle school, high school and college levels. Upon retiring from the classroom, she continued to consult in the areas of teaching writing, editing, and transformational school leadership. Though she always keeps writing and editing for academic publications on her desk, Susie has been, at heart, a lifetime poet. She is active with various poetry organizations and loves the intersection of composing music and lyrics with her poetry writing.

Tamara Belko is a middle school English teacher, gifted intervention specialist and creative writing coach. She has been in education for fifteen years, sharing her love of reading, writing and poetry with her students. Tamara holds a Masters of Education from Ashland University and lives in Rocky River, Ohio with her husband and three children. When she isn't reading or writing, she can be found listening to music or hiking with her family.